Modifying Schoolwork

Teachers' Guides to Inclusive Practices

Modifying Schoolwork

by

Rachel Janney, Ph.D.
Radford University
Radford, Virginia

and

Martha E. Snell, Ph.D.
University of Virginia
Charlottesville

with contributions from

Johnna Elliott, M.Ed.
Cynthia R. Pitonyak, B.S.
Kenna M. Colley, Ed.D.

·P·A·U·L·H·
BROOKES
PUBLISHING Co.®

Baltimore • London • Toronto • Sydney

Paul H. Brookes Publishing Co.
Post Office Box 10624
Baltimore, Maryland 21285-0624

www.brookespublishing.com

Typeset by Barton Matheson Willse and Worthington, Baltimore, Maryland.
Manufactured in the United States of America by Versa Press, East Peoria, Illinois.

All of the vignettes in this book are composites of the authors' actual experiences. In all instances, names have been changed; in some instances, identifying details have been altered to protect confidentiality.

Third printing, February 2002.

Library of Congress Cataloging-in-Publication Data

Janney, Rachel.
   Modifying schoolwork / by Rachel Janney and Martha E. Snell with contributions from Johnna Elliott . . . [et al.].
      p.   cm.—(Teachers' guides to inclusive practices)
   Includes bibliographical references and index.
   ISBN 1-55766-354-8
    1. Inclusive education—United States—Planning.   2. Handicapped children—Education—United States—Planning.   3. Classroom management—United States.   I. Snell, Martha E.
II. Elliott, Johnna.   III. Title.   IV. Series.
LC1201.J26   2000
371.9'046—dc21

                                                   99-43331
                                                   CIP

British Library Cataloguing in Publication data are available from the British Library.

Contents

About the Authors

Rachel Janney, Ph.D., has worked with children and adults with disabilities in a number of capacities, including special education teacher, camp counselor, educational consultant, and researcher. She received her master's degree from Syracuse University and her doctorate from the University of Nebraska–Lincoln. Dr. Janney now teaches courses in special education, supervises student teachers, and coordinates the undergraduate program in special education at Radford University. She also serves as Co-director of the Training and Technical Assistance Center (T/TAC) for Professionals Serving Individuals with Disabilities at Radford University. The T/TAC, part of a statewide technical assistance network that is funded by the Virginia Department of Education, provides a variety of services and resources to special education teams in school divisions throughout southwest Virginia.

Martha E. Snell, Ph.D., is a professor in the Curry School of Education at the University of Virginia where she has taught since 1973. Her focus is special education and, specifically, the preparation of teachers of students with mental retardation and severe disabilities and young children with disabilities. Prior to completing her doctoral degree in special education at Michigan State University, she worked with children and adults with disabilities as a residential child care worker, a teacher, and a provider of technical assistance to school and residential programs. In addition to teaching coursework at the undergraduate and graduate levels, she currently coordinates the special education program, supervises teachers in training, provides in-service training to teachers and parents in schools and agencies, conducts research, serves on the boards of several community agencies serving people with disabilities, and is an active member of the American Association on Mental Retardation and TASH (formerly The Association for Persons with Severe Handicaps).

Dr. Janney and coauthor Dr. Snell have conducted several research projects in inclusive schools and classrooms. These projects have studied the ways that special and general education teachers work together to design and implement adaptations and accommodations for students with disabilities in inclusive settings. Both authors are frequent presenters of workshops on topics related to successful inclusive education.

Johnna Elliott, M.Ed., and Cynthia R. Pitonyak, B.S., are consulting teachers in a school division that serves all students in their neighborhood schools and provides individualized adaptations and accommodations to support students with disabilities within general education classrooms alongside their peers without disabilities. As consulting teachers, they provide and coordinate an array of supports for students across all disability categories.

Kenna M. Colley, Ed.D., previously an elementary school inclusion specialist, is now the lead coordinator for the T/TAC at Radford University in Radford, Virginia. Her current role involves facilitating local school systems' improvement efforts, including enhancing their use of inclusive education practices.

Acknowledgments

This booklet adapts and builds on the work of many other educators, administrators, and parents who have found effective ways to modify schoolwork for students with an array of abilities. We are particularly grateful for the ideas provided by the work of Alison Ford, Michael F. Giangreco, Linda Davern, Bobbi Schnorr, and Alice Udvari-Solner. We also would like to thank Virginia Lewis for her valuable assistance in preparing the manuscript, including the creation of many of the figures used in this booklet.

We would also like to acknowledge our editors at Brookes Publishing: Scott Beeler, who helped get the "booklet concept" off the ground, and Lisa Benson and Kristine Dorman for their excellent editing and persistence in completing this series of booklets.

To all the educators, parents, and students who are working to create and maintain inclusive school environments: places where all students have membership, enjoy social relationships with peers, and have the needed supports to learn what is important for them to be successful in life

Modifying Schoolwork

Chapter 1

Inclusive Programming

The Big Picture

This booklet is designed for use by teams of general and special educators who share responsibility for educating elementary, middle, and high school students with a full range of disabilities who are receiving special education. The booklet has two main purposes: 1) to offer a general framework for making decisions about modifying instructional activities in inclusive classrooms and 2) to provide examples of specific tactics and strategies developed by teachers to design and monitor modifications for individual students. The tools and tactics provided were contributed by teachers in several school districts who have implemented inclusive education practices. Some of these strategies have been adapted from the work of other educators (e.g., The Homecoming Model, Thousand et al., 1986; Syracuse, New York's, inclusive education project, Davern, Ford, Erwin, Schnorr, & Rogan, 1993; Wisconsin School Inclusion Project, Ford et al., 1995). These strategies continue to evolve as they are applied creatively by teams of teachers working with a variety of students.

Although it takes much effort to prepare a school district and its schools to provide effective education in inclusive environments, the primary focus of this booklet is on inclusive strategies for the classroom rather than on strategies for schools or school systems. Issues directly related to "getting in the door" or issues related to moving students from segregated or self-contained classrooms to integrated or inclusive classrooms are not addressed in this booklet, although some helpful references are provided. Also, extensive information about the development of individualized education programs (IEPs) is not provided, even though IEPs for inclusive classrooms may be quite different from those developed for students in self-contained special education classrooms.

Instead, the focus of this booklet is on the process of making modifications for students with IEPs. It is assumed that these students are starting the school year in an inclusive classroom with a teacher who 1) considers each student to be a full member of the class,

2) has the support of a collaborating or consulting special education teacher, and 3) has the assistance of other support personnel as determined by the needs of the student. Chapter 1 gives an overview of some of the broad school and classroom practices that set the stage for effectively educating students in inclusive classrooms. Chapter 2 provides a model for thinking about the process of making modifications—the elements of curriculum, instruction, and setting, all which can be modified. Chapter 3 relates the planning steps required to design and implement individualized adaptations for specific students. Chapter 4 examines team communication, as well as the monitoring and evaluation of students' progress. Chapter 5 presents a number of ideas for adapting instructional activities. Finally, Appendix A provides blank copies of many of the forms that are used throughout this booklet, and Appendix B lists a number of resources that may be consulted for additional information.

Throughout this booklet, each planning format or adaptation strategy is illustrated using composite case examples of actual students we have known. Case examples include students of varying ages with a range of support needs.

KEY COMPONENTS FOR INCLUSIVE EDUCATION

There are six key components to the successful functioning of inclusive education. They are as follows: an inclusive program model, collaborative teaming and problem solving, common goals and values, specific strategies to facilitate peer supports, an inclusive culture in the school, and accommodating curricular and instructional practices in the classroom.

An Inclusive Program Model

In nearly every school district in the United States, teachers, parents, and administrators are discussing issues related to the inclusion of students with disabilities in general education classrooms. People have come to use the

---

What is inclusive education?

✓ Neighborhood schools

✓ All students based in general education homerooms and classes

✓ General and special education teacher consultation and collaboration to incorporate special supports and services into age-appropriate school and community environments

✓ Flexible and individualized decision making about services, supports, and locations for instruction

---

Figure 1.1.   Definition of inclusive education.

terms *inclusive education* or *full inclusion* to describe a variety of special education programming options. This booklet uses these terms to mean providing necessary services and supports for students with disabilities from within a home base of general education classes in neighborhood schools.

According to the definition given in Figure 1.1, inclusive education means that individualized supports follow the student; therefore, students with disabilities are not isolated from their peers without disabilities. This definition also means that participation in general classes is the goal for all students and that decisions about which of a student's needs are addressed outside the classroom are based on the skills to be taught and where instruction to address those skills is best delivered. Such decisions are not based on students' disability classifications. True inclusive education requires collaborative teaming to plan individual student's daily schedules and collabora-

tive instruction and to incorporate special education services and supports into the classroom. It does *not* mean that students no longer receive specialized instruction and related services or that students are thrown into the mainstream to sink or swim (Figure 1.2). After all, the legal definition of special education is "specially designed instruction," a definition that makes no reference to the place where such instruction occurs.

If students with disabilities are not scheduled into a school's general classes before other alternatives are developed on an individualized basis, then revising the program model is the place to start. An inclusive program model means that students with IEPs are placed on general education class rosters but still are provided with an IEP service coordinator and/or consulting teacher who has the required specialized knowledge and competencies. In addition to removing the division between special and general education

---

What the Research Says

Many teachers, parents, and advocates have expressed concern about the effects of part-time mainstreaming on the social relationships among students with and without disabilities. Schnorr (1990) found that first-graders defined their school experience on the basis of themes that centered on sharing the same class assignments, activities, and peer networks. Peter, a student with mental retardation who was mainstreamed part time into this class, was not perceived by peers to be a class member because "he did not share in the first grade experience as defined by these students" (Schnorr, 1990, p. 38). Instead, Peter was perceived as a visitor and had little chance of developing a friendship with the other students because friends, as defined by these students, were members of the same class.

Figure 1.2.   Effects of part-time mainstreaming.

students, creating an inclusive program model means reorganizing the ways teachers and staff are assigned to classrooms. Inclusive schools use a variety of staffing arrangements, including 1) grade-level teams or families, in which a special education teacher provides direct and/or indirect support for the identified students at one or more grade levels; 2) cooperative teaching, in which a general educator and special educator share responsibility for a particular classroom or classrooms; and 3) support or itinerant teacher models, in which several special education teachers serve students with certain disabilities across several classrooms or schools. Paraprofessionals or instructional assistants are also often important team members. The team model that a school adopts has many implications for the ways that modifications are made for students. It determines how much in-class support is provided by the special education teacher, the amount of time available for joint planning, and the way teams share space and other resources.

Collaborative Teaming and Problem Solving

Teaming has always been required as part of the IEP process; however, inclusive education tends to require more ongoing communication and collaboration than other program models. Inclusive programs require general and special education teachers and support staff to share responsibility for educating students with disabilities on a daily basis. This means that teachers' roles must be defined in new ways; one teacher is no longer solely responsible for a classroom of students. The programs require that general and special education teachers work together on a variety of collaborative teams. These team models may include student-centered support teams, grade-level teams, and departmental teams.

Inclusive education also requires that teams know how to communicate, plan, and deliver services jointly. The preparation and planning that must be conducted to enable teachers, parents, and other service providers to work together effectively as a team is addressed in *Collaborative Teaming* (Snell & Jan-

ney, 2000), a companion booklet in this series. One initial step toward improving teaming efforts is to adopt or develop strategies for defining and clarifying team members' roles and responsibilities. The Team Roles and Responsibilities Checklist (Figure 1.3) provides a structure for explicit discussion of questions about which team members will meet which responsibilities. If a classroom is truly inclusive, the special education teacher is *not* the person with primary responsibility for every item on the Team Roles and Responsibilities Checklist. Figure 1.3 shows how staff roles and responsibilities are divided for a first-grade classroom team.

The team also needs to identify processes for making joint decisions about individualized modifications and supports and for communicating decisions among all team members. Chapters 3 and 4 offer many planning and communication strategies that teams can use or adapt. Because inclusive education requires individualization, it is important for teams to take a problem-solving orientation toward their work. Although certain resources can help by providing guidelines and ideas for educating students in inclusive ways, the many differences among children, classrooms, and communities require that teams view their work as an ongoing process of figuring out what works for each student in a particular classroom situation. We cannot overemphasize that inclusive education is an evolutionary process. The question to ask is "How can we make it work in this school for these students?" The answer to that question will change every year.

Common Goals and Values

The decisions we make about modifications depend on our beliefs and values regarding the purpose of education and the benefits of belonging. It may be impossible for a team to agree on the acceptability of curricular and instructional adaptations unless team members agree on certain values, because values become the criteria used to evaluate decisions. For example, the content of this booklet is founded on the belief that all students

Team Roles and Responsibilities Checklist

Classroom _Ramirez/1st_   **Date** _10/24/96_

Teaching and Support Team Members:

Ramirez Classroom Teacher   _O'Donnell_ Instructional Assistant

Pitonyak Special Education Teacher   _____ Other

Key: x = Primary responsibility
       input = Input into decision making and/or implementation

Roles and responsibilities	Who is responsible?			
	Classroom teacher	Special education teacher	Instructional assistant	Other: _____
Developing lessons/units	x	input		
Adapting curriculum	input	x		
Adapting teaching methods	x	x	input	
Adapting materials	input	x	input	
Monitoring student progress	x (daily)	x (reports)	x (data log)	
Assigning grades	x	x		
Assigning duties to/supervising assistants	x (daily)	x (training)		
Scheduling team meetings a. IEP teams b. Core planning teams	x input	input x		
Daily/weekly communication with parents	x	input	input	
Communication/collaboration with related services		x (service coordinator)	input (notes, logs)	
Facilitating peer supports	x	x (peer planning)	input	

Figure 1.3.   Team Roles and Responsibilities Checklist. (From Ford, A., Messenheimer-Young, T., Toshner, J., Fitzgerald, M.A., Dyer, C., Glodoski, J., & Laveck, J. [1995, July]. *A team planning packet for inclusive education.* Milwaukee: Wisconsin School Inclusion Project; adapted by permission.)

should have the opportunity to attend school together and to be treated as full and equal members of their classroom groups and communities. In addition, the practices described in this booklet reflect a belief that adaptations should meet the criteria of facilitating both social and instructional participation and of being "only as special as necessary."

The most effective adaptations are designed to facilitate both social and instructional participation in class activities. That is, learning activities can and should be designed so that students with varying abilities work together within shared activities. One goal of inclusive education is for students with IEPs to be full members of their classes and schools and to participate in the ongoing social life of the class. Another goal is for students to achieve academic and functional competence at whatever level is suitable for them. That is, although it is important for all students to be included with peers in their age group for social purposes, just being present or being included for "socialization" is not enough. It is also important that students make progress toward specific learning goals, whether those goals involve social, academic, motoric, or personal aspects of education.

Therefore, adaptations are ideally designed not only to keep the student busy or present with classmates but also to enable the student to practice and master relevant instructional goals. Students' goals will range from being slightly different to being vastly different from their classmates' curriculum goals. The adaptations designed for students with very different curriculum goals should enable them to take an active part in instructional activities, even if their participation is designed to achieve a different learning outcome than that of their classmates. Teachers may sometimes find themselves questioning the value of adapting an activity that seems to be distant from the functional skill needs of a student with a severe disability; however, they should remember that functionality is only one criterion for selecting IEP goals and objectives. Other valid criteria for selecting learning outcomes include student or family preference, age appropriateness, and the opportunity to increase the student's social participation and interaction. As Kenna Colley, a special education consulting teacher, noted, "Sometimes, the activity should be adapted because it is necessary to the student, even if it does not seem very relevant to the adults" (personal communication, September 10, 1997). The two prior-

ities—social and instructional participation— need to be balanced. At times, teachers may have to make a choice to emphasize one or the other for a particular activity; though, they can also continue to try to figure out how to move closer to accomplishing both.

The most effective adaptations are "only as special as necessary." The adaptations that are created to enable the student to participate in classroom activities should not be more intrusive than necessary. Teachers do not want to conceal individual differences or to pretend that they do not exist. In fact, it is important for students without disabilities to learn to appreciate individual differences and to learn that equality does not require everyone to be treated identically. However, no one wants to be singled out to receive special treatment *all* the time. Furthermore, receiving extra assistance or adapted instruction should not require removing the student from opportunities to engage in typical activities and to develop "ordinary" relationships, such as friendships and acquaintances with a variety of people. Such treatment can interfere with the development of peer acceptance, self-confidence, and independence (Table 1.1).

An "only as special as necessary" approach to adaptations suggests altering only the elements of the lesson or activity necessary to enable the student to participate actively in meeting IEP objectives and altering those elements in the least extraordinary way possible. As Strickland and Turnbull (1990) noted, the specialness or intrusiveness of an adaptation is determined from the student's perspective (Figure 1.4). The ideal is to create adaptations that deviate as little as possible from the ordinary, yet enable the student to benefit from the activity. From the teacher's

Table 1.1.　"Only as special as necessary" approach to adaptations

Student's need for specialization	Student's common ground with others
Adaptive equipment	Regular lives
Related therapy services	Ordinary relationships
Adapted curriculum	Everyday activities
Adapted instruction	Typical places
Specialized methods	Common events

What is another word for *intrusive?* The thesaurus lists synonyms such as *annoying, bothersome, distracting, disturbing,* and *pushy.* When judging the intrusiveness of an adaptation, it may be helpful to ask, "Is this adaptation annoying or bothersome to the student?" or, "Are we being too pushy in making the adaptation this way?" (Strickland & Turnbull, 1990)

Figure 1.4. Intrusiveness of adaptations from the student's perspective.

perspective, this type of adaptation is not always the easiest, as it often requires a change in teacher behavior rather than in what the student does or in the materials provided for the student.

The "only as special as necessary" approach also reminds teachers to not assume that the student needs a teacher or assistant by his or her side every minute or that the goals or materials for each lesson must always be modified. Furthermore, adapting an activity does not require sitting at a table at the back of the room. Adaptations can be provided alongside classmates, within the context of ongoing classroom activities.

It is useful to use agreed-on values as standards for evaluating classroom adaptations and other inclusion efforts. Although it is typical for teams to make unspoken assumptions about team or individual values, *open discussion* of beliefs and values can enhance team effectiveness. One strategy to help generate open discussion about values that support inclusion is to dedicate a faculty meeting to creating or revising the school mission statement to ensure that it includes all students. At the team level, if team members do not share a belief in the value of social and instructional participation, then discussions about values among team members may help the team to agree on key practices that will guide their shared work. For example, the team may be able to agree on the value of hands-on lessons or a language-rich classroom or on the importance of in-class support during reading instruction for students who are having trouble reading. If each team member makes some compromises to reach an agreement about the common practices that are valued by the team, there is a starting

point for collaboration and the development of additional shared values. Another strategy to use when all the teachers in a school do not agree on the value of inclusive education is to start on a smaller scale. For instance, one particular grade level or department that consists of teachers who do value inclusion may define their common values and then pilot an inclusive classroom model for the school based on these values. This sort of example can help other teachers to recognize the benefits of inclusion for students, teachers, and families.

Specific Strategies to Facilitate Peer Supports

Another essential component of inclusive education is the facilitation of support networks among students. A number of strategies have been developed to promote the development of enriching relationships among classmates with and without disabilities. Circles of Friends (Vandercook, York, & Forest, 1989) and other person-centered planning processes (Forest & Lusthaus, 1990; Mount & Zwernik, 1989, 1990; O'Brien, 1987) invite peers to participate in planning and problem solving regarding the needs of a classmate with a disability. Teachers in inclusive classrooms often use adapted versions of such processes to do "peer planning" or "peer problem solving" for all the students in the class rather than for just the students with disabilities. Cooperative learning approaches that emphasize teaching students the social skills needed for effective teaming have also been used to promote equitable student interactions and relationships (Putnam, 1993; Thousand, Villa, & Nevin, 1994). It is important, however, to be sensitive to the possible drawbacks of placing too much focus on peer helping relationships. Students with disabilities also need purely social relationships with their peers and need to be helpers to others rather than always being the ones who are being helped. "We must be careful not to overemphasize the helper-helpee aspect of a relationship. Unless help is reciprocal the inherent inequality between helper and helpee will contaminate the authenticity of the relationship. Friendship is not the same as help" (Van der Klift & Kunc, 1994, p. 393). Strategies for facilitating peer supports and constructive relationships in inclusive classrooms are addressed more fully in *Social Relationships and Peer Support* (Snell & Janney, 2000), another booklet in this series.

An Inclusive Culture in the School

Research on inclusive education suggests that one of the most fundamental ways to promote inclusion is to create a school culture that is anchored in a sense of community and emphasizes the value of diversity (Figure 1.5). Inclusive schools welcome and accommodate all students. Books and journal articles on effective schools and school restructuring emphasize themes that are remarkably consistent with guidelines for creating inclusive schools. For example, to a great extent, effective schools are schools that welcome and capitalize on diversity. Effective schools also tend to have a collaborative culture and a strong sense of community. Figure 1.6 provides a summary of the essential elements of effective and inclusive schools with strategies to help develop each element.

Accommodating Curricular and Instructional Practices in the Classroom

Just as an inclusive school culture is accommodating for all students in the classroom, effective teaching practices also tend to be effective for a range of students. Many students, including students with and without disabilities, are not likely to be successful in traditional general education classrooms with a "one size fits all" approach to curriculum and teaching strategies. *Unaccommodating classrooms* rely heavily on textbook-based curriculum in which every student is expected to be on the same page at the same time, to read aloud repeatedly, and to answer questions at the end of each chapter. Large-group lectures followed by uniform seatwork exercises also are ineffective for many learners.

Other classroom practices tend to be more effective for a range of students. *Accommodating classrooms* are characterized by a climate of warmth and inclusiveness and by curricular and instructional practices that emphasize

---

Voices from the Classroom

 Both Kenna Colley and Cyndi Pitonyak are special education consulting teachers at an elementary school where the principal has successfully created a strong sense of belonging for students, teachers, and parents. Kenna and Cyndi note that this principal attends to the "big picture" and also does little things that count toward making each member of the school community feel valued. Some of the things the principal has done to make people feel noticed and appreciated include the following:

- Bringing food to faculty meetings—the principal provides snacks the first month, then the teachers at each grade level sign up for subsequent months
- Setting a monthly lunch date with parents
- Swapping roles with teachers
- Being part of students' behavior support plans by, for example, regularly visiting a classroom to encourage a particular student
- Acting as a substitute teacher so that teachers have more time to meet
- Getting release time for teachers and instructional assistants to attend in-services
- Putting notes of appreciation and recognition in faculty and staff mailboxes

Figure 1.5.   How one principal builds community.

1. **Administrators who work with teachers to identify a vision,** a clear definition of "who we are" as a school, and who provide leadership for school improvement
   - ✓ Structure opportunities for expression of ideas and values regarding the vision
   - ✓ Solicit input from teachers and parents to articulate a vision and value base
   - ✓ Adjust policies and procedures to reflect vision and values
   - ✓ Provide opportunities for professional development, visitations, and sharing successes
2. **A warm, caring school culture** that emphasizes acceptance of all students, is based in a sense of community and social connectedness, and emphasizes the development of self-direction and concern for others
   - ✓ Schedules all students into regular classes as a home base
   - ✓ Evaluates student performance in ways that allow for individual differences
   - ✓ Creates activities to demonstrate valuing of different characteristics and abilities
   - ✓ Organizes activities to welcome newcomers
   - ✓ Provides opportunities to meet other students, staff, and parents
   - ✓ Initiates community helping activities
   - ✓ Develops peer supports, class meetings, and problem-solving sessions
   - ✓ Surveys and improves accessibility of the building and classrooms
3. **Collaboration and partnerships** among teachers, families, and students
   - ✓ Establish buildingwide planning and problem-solving teams
   - ✓ Brainstorm creative strategies to provide time and opportunities for collaborative planning
   - ✓ Provide staff development on collaborative skills for teachers and students
   - ✓ Adopt a process for clearly defining team roles and responsibilities
   - ✓ Hold regular team meetings around individual students with agendas, assigned roles, and time limits
   - ✓ Implement ongoing home–school communication
4. **High expectations** regarding all students and their abilities
   - ✓ Mastery learning
   - ✓ Portfolio and authentic assessment
   - ✓ Include all students in learning standards
5. **Ongoing staff development and training** to help create a professional culture that is open to experimentation and risk taking
   - ✓ Assess staff development needs
   - ✓ Work with local universities and technical assistance programs to provide training
   - ✓ Incorporate topics, such as curriculum adaptation, behavioral support, and collaboration, into school in-service plan

Figure 1.6.   Creating an effective and inclusive school.

choice, meaning, active learning, and student interaction. They use flexible, fluid groupings and multiple approaches to content and student products, and they emphasize the student as discoverer or constructor of knowledge and the teacher as the facilitator. To the extent that teachers promote and incorporate accommodating curricular and instructional practices, they are also helping to create classrooms where more children with and without disabilities can be successful. In fact, research on effective teaching suggests that it is effective across a range of students (Figure 1.7).

A brief description of some of the accommodating curricular and instructional practices follows. The resource list in Appendix B provides references that serve as sources for these descriptions; they may be consulted for additional information. It is important not to view these practices as prerequisites for inclusive education or to wait until all schools and classrooms are accommodating before providing students with access to general education. In fact, the use of such practices actually makes the task of developing adaptations for individual students easier. In one sense, the least intrusive adaptation is made when teachers adapt their teaching strategies for the entire class. As illustrated in Figure 1.8, the more inclusive the school culture and the more accommodating the classroom, the fewer individualized adaptations required.

What the Research Says

Good and Brophy summarized and reviewed a range of literature on effective teaching practices. They concluded that "There is no dimension of individual difference that has unambiguous implications for instructional method. It seems most appropriate to use principles of instructional design and pedagogy to develop high-quality instructional materials and methods intended to be effective for all students rather than to set out from the beginning to develop different materials and methods for various students" (1991, p. 348).

Figure 1.7.   Effective teaching.

Meaningful, Reality-Based Curriculum
When schoolwork is designed to help students to practice useful skills and achieve real purposes, interest and motivation are increased. Authentic curriculum also enhances learning by helping students to make connections with their prior knowledge and experience, and it assists with generalization and transfer to "real life." Examples of curricular approaches that embody meaning and authenticity include a writer's workshop, in which students use the steps of the writing process to create written documents that achieve purposes they have identified, and community-referenced curriculum, in which students' curriculum objectives and learning activities are identified by inventorying the activities in which they need to participate to be active in their schools and communities.

Integrated, Thematic Curriculum   An integrated or thematic curriculum helps students to make the connections among subject areas that are required outside of school, promotes thinking and problem solving, and provides repeated practice throughout the day. The whole language approach to reading and language arts and thematic or project-based units are examples of integrated curricular approaches. (See Chapter 5 for an example of a format to use for planning thematic units.)

Multicultural Curriculum   Purposefully teaching students about differences and similarities in gender, race, culture, family, and ability supports respect and understanding of individual and group differences. Multicultural curriculum is often paired with thematic and integrated curricular approaches.

Active, Hands-On Teaching and Learning
Activity-based lessons, such as demonstrations, simulations, applied learning stations, role plays, community-based projects, and learning games, help to ensure that students have opportunities to become actively engaged in the learning process. Students with less sophisticated cognitive structures and whose learning style is tactile/kinesthetic especially benefit from interacting with concrete activities. Activities for students with learning and intellectual disabilities must be structured to keep them focused on the purpose and procedures of the activity. Discovery learning using open-ended activities tends to be less beneficial for these students, unless they also receive direct instruction in specific, targeted skills.

Use of a Variety of Flexible, Small Groups
The use of small groups, especially for presenting new skills and material, helps to optimize opportunities for active responding and peer modeling and to ensure that all students

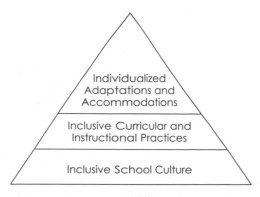

Figure 1.8.   Accommodating schools and classrooms decrease the need for individualized adaptations.

have a chance to make a contribution. Instead of basing all small groups on a fixed decision about the students' abilities, student groupings should be based on a variety of dimensions, depending on the purpose and nature of the task. Groups can be organized on the basis of modality preferences, prerequisite skills, interests, hobbies, and projects. Peer-mediated groups, such as peer tutoring and cooperative learning, are some of the most frequently reported instructional strategies used by teachers in inclusive classrooms. Peer-mediated instruction, often used in combination with activity-based learning and other instructional support strategies, has been reported to reduce the need for multiple adaptations. The effective use of small groups requires teaching students skills for interacting, communicating, and resolving differences.

Systematic Lesson Structure   Although there are numerous models for designing effective learning tasks, most students benefit from lessons that include structuring (purpose, prespecified objectives, review/connect), presentation (information, demonstration or modeling, multiple checks for understanding), sufficient practice (both guided and independent, with progress monitored and feedback provided), closure (review, transition), and application. Research shows that effective teachers teach in small steps and give students a lot of successful practice after each step.

Multiple Modalities   Many learners benefit from activities that use movement, vision, rhythm, and/or social or affective modalities, rather than only from watching, listening, and speaking, which are often the primary modalities for sharing information in classrooms. Especially important is the use of graphics and other visual representations. Although the various taxonomies of learning styles differ in their organizational dimensions, they all point to the need to differentiate instruction by capitalizing on learners' strengths and learning styles.

Strategic Teaching and Learning   Instruction that requires more than memorization helps students to develop the thinking and problem-solving skills needed in the

workplace and in the broader community. Many students benefit from direct modeling and practice of strategies for acquiring, storing, and retrieving information. Explicit instruction in cognitive and metacognitive skills—skills for organizing, storing, and retrieving information—provides students with a better understanding of the demands of learning tasks, the structure of knowledge, and techniques to accelerate their learning.

Regular Monitoring of Performance Using Alternative Assessments   Alternative assessments that allow for continuous progress at individualized rates include portfolios, curriculum-based assessments, anecdotal records, peer-assisted evaluation, self-monitoring, and conferencing with the teacher. In accommodating classrooms, a variety of indicators are used, progress is evaluated over time, and students learn to evaluate themselves.

SURVEYING YOUR SCHOOL'S INCLUSIVE PRACTICES

Developing an effective inclusive education program requires attention to many elements beyond adapting teaching methods and materials. Figure 1.9 is a survey that includes six key ingredients that are important to the process of putting an inclusive philosophy into action. Although the planning for individualized adaptations, which is the main subject of this booklet, is performed by the core team that supports a student or students on a daily basis, this "big picture" checklist can be completed by a grade-level team, a classroom team, or a general inclusion planning team or committee.

Along with the checklist is a problem-solving format that is useful for educational teams that want to work together to improve the inclusive practices in their school. The problem-solving format, known as the Issue-Action Plan (Figure 1.10), is used by many of the teachers who contributed to this booklet. The Issue-Action Plan helps the team to focus on specific issues or problems that need to be solved and on the steps that need to be taken

Team Survey of Inclusive Practices

School _____ Team _____ Year _____

Team Members/Roles:

_____   _____

_____   _____

_____   _____

Status Key: 1 = We have done it well.
                   2 = We have tried, but it needs
                       improvement.
                   3 = We have not done it.

Action Priority: Indicate "high" or "low."
Complete Issue-Action Plan for high-
priority items.

Practice	Status (1, 2, 3)		Action Priority (high/low)	
	Date:	Date:	Date:	Date:
1. **Do we have an inclusive program model?** Do all students start from a base in general classes? Are services and supports pulled in rather than students being pulled out?				
2. **Do we use collaborative team planning and problem-solving strategies?** Have we identified team members' roles and responsibilities? Do we have strategies for making and communicating decisions about adaptations?				
3. **Do we agree about our goals and values?** Do we agree on the value of belonging? Do we want adaptations that facilitate social and instructional participation and are only as special as necessary?				
4. **Does our school have an accommodating culture and climate?** Is diversity valued? Are we a community? Do we expect excellence and equity for all students?				
5. **Does the classroom use accommodating curricular and instructional practices?** Is the curriculum meaningful? Do we use active learning; multiple modalities; and small, flexible groupings?				
6. **Do we have specific strategies to facilitate peer supports?** Do we teach social interaction and problem-solving skills? Do we facilitate social and helping relationships for all students?				

Figure 1.9.   Team survey of inclusive practices. (From Ford, A., Messenheimer-Young, T., Toshner, J., Fitzgerald, M.A., Dyer, C., Glodoski, J., & Laveck, J. [1995, July]. *A team planning packet for inclusive education.* Milwaukee: Wisconsin School Inclusion Project; adapted by permission.)

Student/Team _____ 5th Grade _____ **Date** ___ 11/3/96 ___

Team Members Present ___ Kenna, Maryanne, Ginni, Tim, Sandy ___

RE: ___ Item #2 from "Team Survey of Inclusive Practices": Do we use collaborative team ___
planning and problem-solving strategies? ___

Issue	Planned Action	Who is Responsible
1. Spend too much meeting time on field trips, standardized testing, and so on, instead of on planning individualized adaptations. 2. We are not always following through with the adaptation strategies we establish at meetings.	1. Do a written agenda at each meeting: first half reserved for individual student planning, second half reserved for organizational issues. Need to find or make agenda form; make copies. 2. Spend first few minutes of each meeting reviewing and reporting on action items from last meeting.	1. _Kenna:_ Make/find agenda form; bring copies to meetings. _Everyone:_ Take turns creating agenda and facilitating meetings. 2. _Facilitator:_ Review action items. _Everyone:_ Report on actions taken.

Figure 1.10. Issue-Action Plan.

to solve them. It also ensures that specific team members have been identified to complete an action step by an agreed-upon date.

The process of surveying and evaluating a particular school's inclusive practices involves several steps. At a team meeting, teachers should evaluate the school on each of the six key components. If there is room for improvement on one or more components, they need to decide which component will be an "action priority" at that time. Then, for each issue, they should brainstorm actions that they can take to move toward improving or resolving that issue. It is important to be as specific and concrete as possible. Next, they should evaluate those actions, decide which actions they will take, and then designate a person or people who will be responsible for taking the action and a timeline for the action. After the action has been implemented for a period of time (e.g., a month, grading period, semester), the team can reevaluate the component on the second "Status" and "Action Priority" columns of the Team Survey of Inclusive Practices form.

For example, the team that completed the Issue-Action Plan in Figure 1.10 rated itself as a "2—We've done it, but it needs improvement" on item number two—the use of collaborative team planning and problem-solving strategies. Two team members noticed that team meetings that were held to discuss planning lesson adaptations for individual students were actually being used to address upcoming field trips and the state-mandated standardized testing program. Another issue centered on team members failing to implement some of the adaptation strategies that had been developed at team meetings. The team brainstormed ways to collaborate more effectively and to increase individual accountability for implementing team decisions. They evaluated the ideas to determine which were the most feasible and productive.

The actions the team decided on were 1) to establish a written agenda at the beginning of each team meeting, 2) to make reporting on action responsibilities that had been accomplished since the last meeting the first item on the agenda, and 3) to reserve the first half of

Voices from the Classroom

Kenna Colley, a special education consulting teacher, helped to establish an Inclusion Committee at her elementary school to aid the principal and teachers in identifying and addressing issues related to supporting teachers and students in inclusive classrooms. The committee meetings were held on the first Monday of every month and were open to anyone who wanted to attend. At the beginning of each meeting, the group would count the number of people present and divide that number into 60 minutes—the time limit for the meetings—to determine how much time each person would be allotted on the agenda. Participants had to agree to come to the meeting prepared to present an issue by telling exactly what they needed. After each issue was presented, the group engaged in problem solving. If the issue was related to needed equipment, resources, or staff time, someone would agree to discuss the issue with the appropriate administrator. If the issue was teacher related, the group's goal was to give that teacher five or six ideas with which to leave the meeting. The Inclusion Committee is no longer in operation because the issues that it addressed have become general school issues (e.g., How do we meet the needs of students with reading difficulties?) rather than issues that are specific to the inclusion of students with disabilities at the school (e.g., How do we meet the needs of students with IEPs who have reading difficulties?).

Figure 1.11.   The Inclusion Committee.

each meeting for individual student planning before addressing administrative and organizational issues. Then, the team designated a person or people who would be responsible for taking each action and for developing a timeline for the action. For example, one team member volunteers to find or create an agenda form and to be responsible for gathering agenda items and recording them on the form. Another team member offers to record decisions, responsibilities, and timelines on the Issue-Action Plan form and to copy and distribute the forms to the rest of the team. Figure 1.11 provides an example of the way in which another school conducted its Inclusion Committee meetings.

Chapter 2

A Model for Making Adaptations

This chapter describes a model for adapting schoolwork in inclusive classrooms. The model includes three types of adaptations: 1) curricular (content and objectives), 2) instructional (methods and materials), and 3) ecological (the environment). The model also involves making adaptations in two stages: general adaptations that stay in place for a period of time and specific adaptations that vary from day to day.

WHAT IS A MODEL AND WHY IS IT NECESSARY?

A *model* for making adaptations is a framework for thinking about the process of designing individualized adaptations. A model can be useful because it enables teachers to view the process in a way that allows them to apply it to a variety of individual students. To illustrate the need for a model, think of a typical instructional activity in most elementary school classrooms, such as oral reading groups. It would not take long to brainstorm dozens of ways to modify reading groups: read an easier book, provide a large-print book, decrease the number of students in the group, assign shorter passages to read, schedule a shorter period of time, increase the amount of time spent in preparation for reading, and so forth. However, the challenge of adapting schoolwork is not simply in generating ideas but in the selection of adaptations that are appropriate for individual students and feasible within a given classroom situation.

A second reason for having a model for making adaptations relates to the need for collaboration in inclusive classrooms. No longer is one teacher responsible for planning, teaching, and evaluating instruction for an entire class. Now, one or more teachers, along with one or more additional staff members, may share these responsibilities. Teamwork can be hindered when team members have not clarified the steps involved in doing their work, such as determining who will do which steps and how decisions will be made. Having a model helps teams to discuss their work using a common language.

THE DIFFERENCE BETWEEN ACCOMMODATIONS AND ADAPTATIONS

The term *accommodations* is used to refer to modifications that are documented by the eligibility process and specified in a student's individualized education program (IEP). Accommodations are changes others make to assist the student. They are provided to enable the student to gain access to the classroom or the curriculum. Accommodations might include giving the student extra time to complete a test, allowing the student to sit close to the chalkboard, or providing the student with a quiet place to study.

Adaptations are changes to learning task requirements, such as changes to the instructional content, teaching methods and materials, or physical environment. Often, these changes are temporary or reduced over time. Examples of adaptations include teaching a student to use a calculator instead of paper and pencil for mathematical computations or requiring a student to demonstrate a targeted social skill rather than write an essay describing what he or she would do in a hypothetical situation.

It is important for all team members who work with a student to be aware of the accommodations for which a student qualifies and to understand that decisions about learning objectives and accommodations are made by the IEP team and documented on the IEP. This information is available prior to many of the decisions that need to be made on a semester-long, weekly, or daily basis about how specific lessons and activities will be adapted. In other words, IEP objectives and accommodations are givens that must be considered when deciding how to make further adaptations. These adaptations, including the specific ways that an adapted curriculum will be coordinated or integrated with the general class curriculum, are determined through on-going team planning based on the parameters provided by the IEP.

THE MODEL: THREE TYPES OF ADAPTATIONS

Every lesson or activity has several elements that can be adapted so that a student can participate in a way that is personally meaningful. Our model organizes these elements into three major categories of adaptations: curricular, instructional, and ecological (Figure 2.1). Knowing the types of adaptations that a student needs can help the team to know when and how to plan the student's adaptations and to keep the adaptations from becoming too intrusive.

Curricular Adaptations

In an inclusive classroom, the scope and sequence of the curriculum are broadened to accommodate a greater range of student learning goals. The traditional general education curriculum includes the following:

- Basic skills (reading, writing, math)
- Content areas
- The arts
- Physical education

To accommodate learners with exceptional needs, the curriculum in an inclusive classroom also includes the following:

- Functional skills for use in daily life at home, at school, and in the community
- Functional academic skills (e.g., money, counting, time) needed to perform daily routines
- Social, communication, and motor skills that are used across the day in a variety of different activities, subjects, and places (These *related* or *embedded skills* are also referred to as *cross-environmental skills* [e.g., Giangreco, Cloninger, & Iverson, 1998].)

It would be ideal to imagine a school in which all students participate in whatever areas and levels of inclusive curriculum are appropriate for them. However, in actuality, we usually think of curriculum adaptation as a change to the traditional general education curriculum. The typical general education curriculum can be adapted in three ways to meet the individual needs of students—by supplementing, simplifying, or altering the curriculum (Figure 2.2).

Supplementary Curriculum Some students with IEPs participate fully in the general education curriculum but require supplementary instruction in one or more subject or

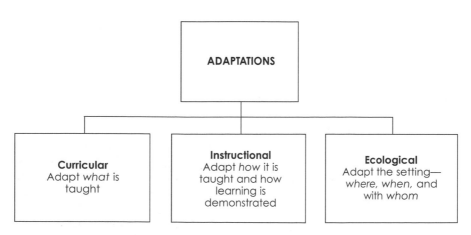

Figure 2.1.   Types of adaptations.

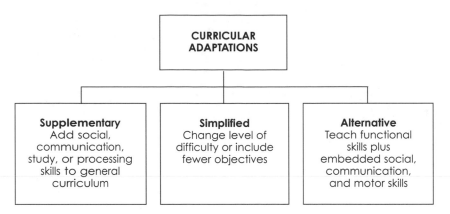

Figure 2.2.   Curricular adaptations.

goal areas. Typical areas for supplementary instruction include basic skills (e.g., reading, writing, math) or skills that are applied across the day (e.g., social skills, study skills, learning strategies). Students whose curricular objectives are adapted primarily by supplementing the general education curriculum would most often be those students identified as having a learning disability or an emotional or behavioral disorder rather than those who have an intellectual disability or severe multiple disabilities. Students identified as having exceptional talents might also participate in supplementary curriculum areas.

Student Snapshot

Troy is a 17-year-old senior in high school. He is enrolled in advanced placement sections of government, biology, and trigonometry but has a learning disability in reading and written language. He has two resource/tutorial sessions per day. He uses the time these sessions provide to complete tests and assignments and to receive instruction and assistance in doing written assignments. Troy participates fully in an advanced academic curriculum with supplementary curriculum adaptations in writing processes and study skills. Virtually all of the modifications made to his instruction are actually accommodations that provide him with extra time, copies of teachers' notes or note-taking assistance, a laptop computer for taking notes, books on tape, oral testing for essay questions, and no penalties for spelling and grammar errors on in-class work. Beyond these special services and his IEP accommodations, Troy requires virtually no ongoing adaptations.

Simplified Curriculum   Other students with IEPs participate in the traditional subject areas, but their work is adapted by teaching simplified objectives or by teaching their objectives at a different level of Bloom's (1976) taxonomy of learning objectives (e.g., some students' objectives might require them to memorize facts or to apply a concept, whereas other students might have objectives requiring analysis or evaluation of the material). Curriculum can also be simplified by emphasizing fewer skills and concepts rather than the entire scope of the general curriculum.

Student Snapshot

Sam is 14 years old and a ninth grader at his local high school. He is a highly articulate young man who has characteristics of pervasive developmental disorder and obsessive-compulsive disorder. Sam has a wide range of academic skills; his vocabulary skills, reading compre-

hension, and general knowledge are his strengths, whereas he finds math and other skill areas that require close attention and decision making to be more challenging. Sam's schedule includes general-level academic courses and electives that allow Sam to explore vocational options. Sam receives full-time special education instruction and support, including six periods per day of pull-in support from a special education teacher or assistant and one period per day of direct instruction in a resource setting. Curriculum adaptations for Sam involve simplifying the content by eliminating technical, conceptually difficult, or confusing material. Because of his curricular modifications, Sam will be a candidate for an IEP diploma rather than an academic diploma.

Alternative Curriculum A third approach to curriculum adaptation involves changing to an alternative, functional curriculum (Ford, Schnorr, Davern, Meyer, Black, & Dempsey, 1989; Peterson, LeRoy, Field, & Wood, 1992). Such a curriculum emphasizes the skills needed to participate in priority activities in the community-living domains of general community use and domestic, self-management, recreational, and vocational skills. We include school as one of the community-living domains, because a community-referenced curriculum is determined by assessing the environments in which a student participates, and school-age students spend a significant portion of their day at school. A functional, community-referenced curriculum also includes the functional academic skills (e.g., reading, writing, money and time management) needed to participate in activities in the community-living domains. For some students, emphasis is placed on the motor, social, and communication skills that will increase their participation in targeted school and community activities (see Rainforth, York, & Macdonald, 1992).

Even students with the most severe disabilities can partially participate in most of the ongoing routines and activities in a typical classroom. Indeed, one of the most common adaptations made for students who have se-

vere or multiple disabilities is to apply the *principle of partial participation* (Baumgart et al., 1982). This principle suggests that individuals who have disabilities should not be deprived of opportunities to participate in typical school and community activities simply because they cannot participate fully or independently in those activities. In other words, a student may not be able to do every part of an activity but that does not mean that some level of participation in that activity would not be valuable to the student.

Student Snapshot

 Daniel, a first-grade student, has multiple disabilities, including cerebral palsy and mental retardation. He can speak a few words, and he has some purposeful movement of his arms and hands but needs physical assistance to perform most daily living and self-help activities. He can take several steps with assistance, but a wheelchair is his primary means of transportation. Daniel's alternative curriculum adaptations emphasize embedded motor and communication skills, partial participation in self-help routines and group activities, and some simplified reading and arithmetic objectives. Rather than providing a separate functional or community-based instruction program, Daniel's instruction in functional skills and routines is integrated into the general education program. Because of Daniel's physical needs, an assistant is assigned to the classroom throughout the day. The assistant positions Daniel in a variety of ways to keep him comfortable and close to his peers and provides the physical assistance that he needs to find objects and to orient himself.

Choosing Appropriate Curriculum Adaptations The distinction among these three approaches to modifying curriculum can aid the adaptation process in several ways. First, the terms can help team members to communicate about the ways they adapt curriculum for individual students. Knowing whether a student's objectives in a particular course or subject area will be supplemented, simplified, or altered can help to clarify the relationship between the student's learning objectives and those of his or her classmates. This does not mean that students should be tracked into a particular type of curriculum adaptation. The type of curriculum adaptation required may vary by subject or skill area and may also vary depending on factors such as the student's age and interests (i.e., high-interest subjects may require fewer adaptations). Different subject areas or different parts of the day may be adapted differently as well. However, teachers may tend to use one type of adapted curriculum for a particular student at a particular point in time. For example, Sam's IEP team has noted that as Sam nears graduation, he will continue to participate in simplified content area instruction but will spend increasing amounts of time in vocational settings. Therefore, his IEP objectives will reflect more functional applications of his academic skills.

Second, the distinction among these three ways to adapt curriculum helps us to keep adaptations "only as special as necessary." Within the context of a given instructional activity, supplementary or simplified curriculum objectives are typically less intrusive than are altered objectives. The use of multilevel curriculum (students working on shared activities but with objectives of varying degrees of difficulty) and curriculum overlap (students working on shared activities but with objectives drawn from different goal areas) is discussed in Chapter 5.

Student Snapshot

Melanie, a fourth grader, has autism. She reads well; writes some words and phrases using a computer; and communicates through a combination of words, gestures, and symbols. Her curricular adaptations involve a combination of simplified objectives in math and language arts

as well as altered, functional objectives in the areas of school routines, self-help, and communication. Therefore, at some times during the day, Melanie works on the same objectives as her classmates, except at a different level. For instance, when her classmates are using the writing process to write book reports, Melanie might write a brief book report on the computer by completing a form developed by the special education teacher, or she may be focusing on the communication, social, and self-management skills that will enable her to function more independently in her school and community. If the group work continues for longer than Melanie is able to effectively participate, she might then use the computer to write a note about her school day for her take-home journal. Melanie also takes several preventive movement "breaks" and has opportunities to use self-calming strategies when necessary to lower her frustration level and to help her to stay focused.

Instructional Adaptations

Instructional adaptations involve changing the way in which the teacher teaches and/or the way the student practices or demonstrates learning. That is, you may change the *instructional stimulus* (input) or change the *student response* (output) (Figure 2.3).

Adapting the Instructional Stimulus or Input The instructional stimulus is the information provided during a lesson or the directions and materials provided for a student during a practice or evaluation activity. The instructional stimulus includes both the content and level of difficulty and the way that the information is provided. For example, during a unit on reptiles, instructional stimuli might include a lecture, a textbook chapter, and oral directions for how to complete a research project. The nature and complexity of the material, the readability of the books, and the clarity of the lecture and directions are all aspects of the instructional stimuli.

Following are some examples of the ways the instructional stimulus or input can be adapted:

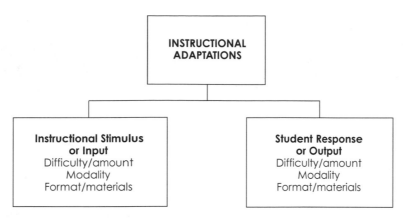

Figure 2.3.   Instructional adaptations.

Level of difficulty/amount

- In oral presentations, use controlled vocabulary and omit extraneous detail.

- Rewrite text passages or test directions at a lower readability level.

- Provide more cues, prompts, and feedback as a student completes practice activities.

- Lecture in brief, 10-minute intervals.

- For each textbook chapter for a content area class, provide a study guide of key concepts and vocabulary terms.

- Reduce the number of problems per page on a math assignment or test.

Modality

- Read text aloud to students.

- Accompany oral information with overheads, graphic organizers, maps, or outlines.

- Provide audio- or videotapes to accompany textbooks.

- Provide models and demonstrations.

Format/materials

- Conduct demonstrations, role plays, and simulations.

- Highlight a content area textbook—yellow for vocabulary words, blue for definitions.

- Provide large-print materials.

- Provide answer boxes or more room to write on tests and worksheets.

- Add pictures or symbols to text.

Adapting the Student Response or Output
The student response, or output, is the behavior that is required of the student. The student response might be listening to a lecture and taking notes, orally answering questions about a videotape, reading a textbook chapter, writing an essay, computing the answers to word problems, constructing a clay pot, or preparing a snack. For example, in a unit on reptiles, student responses might include listening to a lecture, reading resource books, taking notes, organizing and writing information in an outline format, and taking a multiple-choice test. Some examples of adaptations to the student response include the following:

Level of difficulty/amount

- Complete only the two-digit multiplication problems on a page of two- and three-digit problems.

- Circle numerals named by the teacher rather than computing the problems on a math assignment.

- Read the same novel written at a lower readability level.

- Work only the odd-numbered word problems on a homework assignment.

- Take notes during a lecture using a slot note format (see **Figure** 5.6).
- Complete only selected steps of an art or science project.

Modality

- Listen to someone else read a test aloud rather than reading it silently.
- Give oral rather than written responses to reading comprehension questions (or vice versa).
- Use an electronic communicator rather than spelling words orally.

Format/materials

- Solve functional math problems rather than practicing isolated skills (e.g., hand out pencils to classmates rather than counting plastic counters to demonstrate one-to-one correspondence).
- Complete a chart, map, or outline instead of writing an essay about a novel.

In a given activity, the instructional stimulus, the student response, or both can be adapted. For example, a student who has visual impairments may need math worksheets with fewer problems written in larger type on each page (adaptation of the instructional stimulus). A student with mental retardation may need a math worksheet that also has fewer problems per page written in larger type (adaptation of the instructional stimulus). These problems also may need to be single-digit addition problems rather than the two-digit addition problems on which classmates are working (adaptation of the student response).

Choosing Appropriate Instructional Adaptations This distinction between adaptations to the instructional stimulus and adaptations to the student response provides teachers with another way to keep adaptations "only as special as necessary." Although the intrusiveness of a particular adaptation will sometimes depend on the student and the situation, some adaptations clearly are more

intrusive than others. *In general, adapting what the teacher and other support personnel do is less intrusive than adapting what the student does.* If the teacher adapts the instructional stimulus by giving clearer directions, using visuals, and creating materials that are suitable for all students, it is less intrusive than adapting the student response by having the student complete individually adapted materials or an altogether different activity. Likewise, if a teacher reads the math word problems on a test aloud to the entire class, the test does not have to be written at a lower readability level for particular students.

Ecological Adaptations

Other adaptations involve modifying the environment rather than the curriculum or the instruction. The purpose of ecological adaptations is to enable a student with social, behavioral, or emotional needs to cope with the demands of the environment while learning new skills. Examples of ecological adaptations include modifying the *place,* the *schedule,* or the number of *people* in the environment (Figure 2.4). Ecological adaptations are not extensively addressed in this booklet because they are most often used as part of behavioral support plans, which are examined in the companion booklet, *Behavioral Support* (Janney & Snell, 2000).

Where: Change the place

- Provide access to privacy for a student who has difficulty concentrating or maintaining equilibrium (e.g., a study carrel, a trip to a private office).
- Place the student's desk in a strategic place (e.g., out of high-traffic areas, away from particular peers, near the teacher's desk, near the chalkboard).

When: Change the schedule

- Adapt the daily schedule to provide additional breaks.
- Find opportunities for a student to spend extra time with preferred adults or peers.

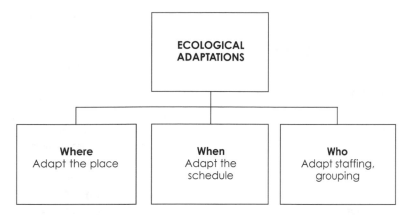

Figure 2.4.   Ecological adaptations.

Who: Change the people

• Use a different teacher for a particular subject or activity.

• Reduce the adult-to-student ratio.

• Change the number of peers with whom the student is grouped for instruction.

Creating Appropriate Ecological Adaptations   One way to keep ecological adaptations as unintrusive as possible is to think of them as supports that are provided for students to help them to be successful. The support will often be temporary or will be faded out over time as the student acquires new competencies to cope with challenges. Receiv-

ing too much support interferes with the development of self-control and self-determination as does receiving too little support.

STAGES OF ADAPTATIONS

One difficulty teachers may encounter while designing adaptations is determining ways to make the task manageable so that they are not always "winging it." A helpful strategy to consider is to break the process down into two stages (Figure 2.5). In the first stage, the team determines which adaptations can be planned for and used for a period of time. This first stage involves creating *general adaptations*. Next, adaptations that are required for specific les-

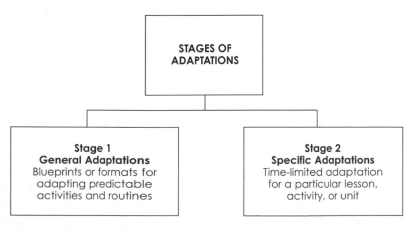

Figure 2.5.   Stages of adaptations: General and specific.

sons or activities can be designed on a weekly or daily basis. These *specific adaptations* are unique, time-limited adaptations designed for a particular lesson, activity, or unit.

General Adaptations

General adaptations are based on the assumption that most classrooms operate according to somewhat predictable patterns. Teachers tend to have an established schedule of daily routines, to use particular instructional formats repeatedly, and to give students certain types of assignments or tasks. Because of these predictable patterns, lessons and activities often can be adapted in similar ways for a period of time. We refer to these adaptations as *general adaptations.* (Some special education teachers prefer to call these *global adaptations;* other teachers might use the term *routine adaptations.*) General adaptations are patterns or formats for adaptations that mirror the predictable routines and instructional activities used in the classroom. They can be planned in advance and used repeatedly.

For example, in elementary classrooms, there is typically a predictable morning routine that includes putting away belongings, taking lunch count, saying the pledge of allegiance, and so forth. During this time, Daniel, the first-grade student with multiple disabilities, puts away his belongings with physical support from an instructional assistant. Next, the class does the "morning letter" routine, which involves identifying a letter of the alphabet, naming things that start with that letter, and then copying the letter and words on paper. Daniel's task is to stamp his name on his morning letter sheet and to color a picture of something that starts with the morning letter. Following the morning letter routine, the teacher gives the students a prompt to use as the topic of their daily journal entry. During journal writing, another predictable activity, Daniel uses an electronic communicator to choose a classmate to assist him with cutting and pasting a picture in his journal. This student also will record a comment about the picture into Daniel's communicator so that

Daniel can play it back during share time later in the morning.

During this sequence of morning activities, Daniel's curricular objectives (putting away his belongings, using his name stamp, and using his electronic communication system) are predictable. The instructional adaptations, which include the prompting routine used by the assistant and most of the adapted materials for his journal entry, also remain the same from day to day. The ecological adaptations (the physical positioning by the assistant) also are performed on a regular, daily basis. All of these general adaptations have been planned by Daniel's team and are described in Classroom Participation Plans (described in Chapter 3), which were written by the special education teacher.

General adaptations may also be developed in middle or high school for subjects or courses where certain instructional formats and activities are used consistently. For example, Sam's ninth-grade World Geography teacher often begins the lesson with a lecture, which typically includes demonstrations and practice in using map reading skills. On at least 2 days each week, the remainder of the class is spent with the students working on projects in cooperative groups. During the lecture, Sam takes notes using a slot note format (i.e., he fills in the blanks on pages of lecture notes that have been prepared for him by the special education teacher). He then joins his cooperative group, which includes peers who Sam knows well. Sam fills the role of "checker" in his group; he is responsible for maintaining a record sheet showing the group's progress toward completion of their project. Periodically throughout the class period, the general education teacher and special education support person, who assists in the class, monitor Sam to ensure that he knows what to do next. The general adaptations for Sam's World Geography class include 1) the format of his slot notes, 2) extra monitoring from the two teachers, 3) placing Sam with particular peers for the cooperative activity, and 4) his standing role as "checker" in the cooperative group.

Once general adaptations, such as those described, have been designed for Daniel and Sam, the same general adaptation "blueprints" can be used repeatedly. Planning for these adaptations requires knowledge of classroom routines, instructional formats, and student objectives and support needs. However, once designed and communicated to the team, many general adaptations can be implemented with minimal day-to-day planning. The content of general adaptations, such as Sam's slot notes and his specific contributions to the cooperative group project, must reflect the week's specific topic; however, the general format for how the class activities are adapted for Sam remains constant for some time.

Specific Adaptations

Although general adaptations can be designed for these predictable classroom routines and instructional formats, the specific curriculum objectives addressed change daily, weekly, or monthly. This means that adaptations that relate to specific content or skills need to vary accordingly. Also, some adaptations may vary because they are required during a new activity or during an activity that is only performed periodically. Adaptations that must vary according to lesson content or structure are called *specific adaptations*. In contrast with general adaptations, specific adaptations require short-term planning between the classroom teacher and special education staff.

For example, the pictures that Daniel colors on his morning letter page are of objects that begin with the particular letter that the class is studying. If Tuesday's morning letter is *r*, Daniel colors a picture of a rabbit that the assistant has found and photocopied onto Daniel's morning letter worksheet. Daniel's classroom teacher and special education teacher (or assistant) need to share information about the morning letter because special education support staff have agreed to be responsible for preparing the appropriate pictures for Daniel to color. In Sam's World Geography class, although the teacher uses a fairly routine set of activities for most class sessions, the topic of the lessons varies from week to week. Therefore, the specific content that Sam learns varies according to the class unit topic. One week it may be regions of the African desert, the next week it might be how mountains are formed. Making content-related adaptations requires weekly communication and joint planning between the World Geography teacher and the special education teacher. They must discuss the lesson content so that Sam's slot notes and his contribution to the cooperative group project can be prepared.

Why Distinguish Between General and Specific Adaptations?

The distinction between general and specific adaptations allows teachers to break down the planning into two stages: The first stage focuses on getting general adaptations into place, and the second stage focuses on creating specific adaptations. Planning is also facilitated by being aware that the type of *curriculum adaptation* used for a student can help to predict whether the student will tend to need more general or specific adaptations. *Students whose curriculum objectives are simplified versions of the general class objectives will tend to need more specific adaptations.* This is because their curriculum content varies according to the content of class lessons. In contrast, students whose curriculum objectives have been altered to a functional curriculum will tend to need more general adaptations because their curriculum content is less determined by the general education content. The specific adaptations developed for students with altered curriculum objectives primarily focus on keeping the student connected with the topics and themes being studied by classmates.

The routine nature of many classroom activities makes developing adaptations a bit less demanding than if the class schedule and the way teachers teach varies extensively from day to day. An approach to making adaptations that take advantage of this aspect of classroom life also fits with classroom teachers' approach to planning because they tend to plan in terms of content and activities,

What the Research Says

Potter (1992) studied the contrast between the ways that special education and general education teachers tend to plan. She noted that general education teachers, faced with large groups of students and a standardized curriculum, tend to focus more on creating tasks. That is, they select the content to "cover" and then plan the routines or activities in which students will be involved. In contrast, special education teachers who deal with smaller numbers of students tend to use a "means–end" planning model that begins by specifying objectives and then organizing learning activities.

Potter suggested that asking a classroom teacher to adapt to the needs of students with disabilities by creating entirely new classroom routines and instructional procedures may be overwhelming at first. Therefore, it may be best to begin by "finding ways to incorporate the student's needs into the existing classroom routines. . . .The more quickly routines can be re-developed, the sooner the teacher will [be able to] deal with the more complex aspects of the student's integration. Also, if a student is not included in normal classroom routines, he or she is not really part of the classroom unit and a major goal of integration is lost" (pp. 123–124). She urged special educators to remember that the classroom teacher is more likely to plan around activities than to plan around objectives. An important function of the special educator's role is to keep the integrated student's goals and objectives in mind when planning with the classroom teacher about how activities can be adapted for the student.

Figure 2.6. How teachers plan.

rather than planning from individualized objectives as special educators are taught to do (Figure 2.6). The planning processes suggested in Chapter 3 build on this concept.

EVALUATING THE "SPECIALNESS" OF ADAPTATIONS

One way to evaluate the adaptations that have been developed is to check them against a list of types of adaptations organized in order from least to most special. The list, provided in Figure 2.7, is generally consistent with suggestions made by other educators who have developed materials on modifications in inclusive classrooms (e.g., Giangreco et al., 1998; Strickland & Turnbull, 1990; Udvari-Solner, 1994). As a general rule, adapting teacher behavior is less intrusive than adapting what the student does (Figure 2.8). The adaptations model, previously described in this chapter, provides a framework for thinking about *which* aspects of a lesson—curriculum, instruction, or ecology—should be adapted (see Figure 2.9).

1. Adapted instruction
    1.1.   Adapted input or instructional stimulus
    1.2.   Adapted output or student response
2. Adapted curriculum
    2.1.   Simplified and/or supplementary curriculum
    2.2.   Altered, functional curriculum
3. Alternative activity with same theme
    3.1.   After or before part of the class activity
    3.2.   With peers
    3.3.   Without peers

Figure 2.7. Hierarchy of adaptations: Least special to most special.

What the Research Says

One way to evaluate the specialness of adaptations is to check them against classmates' perceptions. Several research studies showed that students without disabilities accept the need for adaptations for their classmates who have disabilities and do not necessarily find adaptations to be unfair or stigmatizing. The important element seems to be creating adaptations that enable the student to participate in ongoing classroom activities. Janney and Snell (1997) found support for this theory in a study of the peer supports used in several inclusive elementary classes. Peers in these classrooms could describe the sorts of adaptations provided for their classmates with moderate and severe disabilities but still viewed these classmates as doing "the same work." For example, when asked, "Does Peter [a student with mental retardation] do the same work?" a classmate replied, "He does the same thing, but he doesn't write that much." In fact, Peter did very little reading or writing, but he did focus on functional academic tasks within activities that were quite similar to those of his classmates.

Figure 2.8. Classmates' perspectives on adaptations.

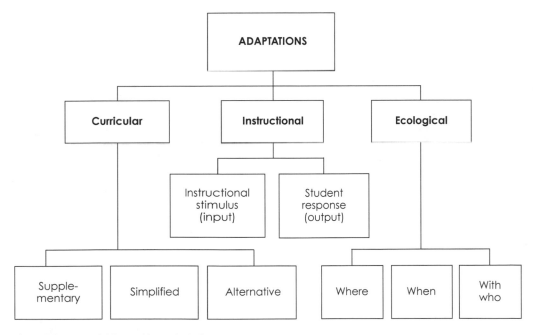

Figure 2.9. A model for making adaptations.

Chapter 3

Planning Adaptations
for Individual Students

This chapter describes the steps and tools of planning individualized adaptations for students (Figure 3.1). It is important to reemphasize that this is a collaborative process and that adaptation strategies are generated and evolve as the team works together. The planning forms illustrated in the chapter should, of course, be adapted by each team to fit the specific needs of the students as well as the planning style of the teacher. Although the process is presented in a sequence of six steps, in reality, the steps may overlap or occur in a somewhat different order, depending on the circumstances. The most fundamental first step is ensuring that the student is connected with peers through a range of social interactions and that he or she is treated as a full and equal member of the classroom group.

Three students who have a range of abilities and support needs are used throughout this chapter as examples to illustrate the adap-

tation planning process. The three students, first introduced in Chapter 2, are Daniel, a first-grader with severe multiple disabilities; Melanie, a fourth-grade student with autism; and Sam, a ninth-grader with emotional and behavioral difficulties. It is impossible to illustrate how each step of the planning process can be used for each school level and every student; therefore, these three students are used to illustrate some of the key ways that the adaptation planning process varies across the age span and across varying levels of support.

Although this chapter focuses on planning adaptations for individual students, a particular team, or various members of several teams, may actually serve several students with individualized education programs (IEPs) in the same classroom. Some strategies to assist in planning for multiple students are described in the companion booklet, *Collaborative Teaming* (Snell & Janney, 2000).

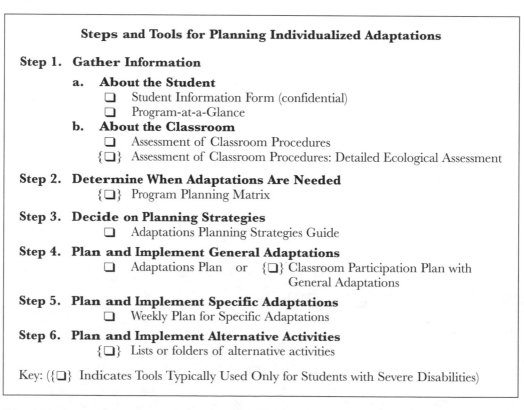

Figure 3.1.   Steps and tools for planning individualized adaptations.

Step 1
Gather Information
About the Student
and the Classroom

 The first step in the adaptation process is to gather and share information that will assist the classroom teacher, special education teacher, instructional assistants, and other team members to create a good fit between the student and the classroom (Figure 3.2). This requires gathering information to assist the team in getting to know the student and getting to know the demands of the classroom. Essentially, the team needs to answer three questions:

1. What are the demands of the classroom?

2. Where is the student now?

3. What adaptations will improve the fit between the student and the classroom and also ensure belonging and achievement?

Information About the Student

What information does the team need to know about the student? In addition to knowing what instructional goals are appropriate for the student, the team also needs to have a sense of who the student is and what "works" for the student. As early as possible in the school year, the special education service coordinator should assemble a packet of information about the student for the classroom teacher and other team members. The amount and type of information required will vary depending on the student, but a two-page, front-to-back form combining a Student Information Form and a Program-at-a-Glance will most likely be needed for each student with an IEP.

Student Information Form   The Student Information Form includes information that will be helpful in determining appropriate programming for the student. The form includes a list of the student's special education and related services, medical/health information, interests, and a summary of what works and does not work with the student. It is best to share this information initially in a face-to-face meeting of the core team so that any additional questions can be asked and answered. The general education teacher keeps the Student Information Form, with only the student's initials on it, in a grade book or other convenient but private place. Figure 3.3 shows a Student Information Form for Melanie, the fourth-grade case study student.

For students with severe disabilities and extensive support needs, the team will probably

---

Voices from the Classroom

Kenna Colley, a special education consulting teacher, states that one of the keys to designing adaptations that work is to build on the things that each classroom teacher does well. That is, "The general education teacher needs to be central in the decision-making about adaptations, or you may end up planning wonderful adaptations that are not compatible with that teacher's teaching methods." For example, one teacher used "literature circles" in which small groups of students discussed each novel that was read. At first, Kenna would plan alternative activities for Melanie to work on during literature circles, such as building a 3-D model to illustrate the novel. Kenna saw that working on these alternative activities meant that Melanie missed out on frequent opportunities for interactions with classmates and reinforcement of the novel content. As a result, she instead provided the classroom teacher with suggestions about ways to enable Melanie to contribute to the literature circle discussion. The hands-on activities that Kenna had been planning solely for Melanie were used as part of a learning center that provided students with a variety of extension activities related to the current novel.

Figure 3.2. Adaptations that work.

Student Information Form (Confidential)

Student _Melanie_   **Grade** _4_   **School Year** _1996–1997_

Current Teachers _Pitonyak and Ramirez_   **Last Year's Teachers** _Fuller and Roberts_

Special Education & Related Services	Likes
✔ Academics (list) *all areas*	*Reading picture books and magazines*
	Computer for writing
	Her space: a place for her things, room to move around
✔ Speech: *20 minutes x 3 days*	
✔ Occupational Therapy: *20 minutes x 1 day*	**Dislikes**
___ Physical Therapy:	*Loud noises*
✔ Aide Support: *5 hours x 5 days*	*Being read to without book to follow along*
✔ Sp. Ed. Instruction: *1/2 hour x 5 days*	*Peanut butter, grape juice, catsup!*
✔ Sp. Ed. Consultation: *1 hour per week*	*Being confined or cramped*
✔ Other:	
Medical/health	**See guidance counselor/ principal for other relevant confidential information?**
	✔ yes ___ no
	Behavior Plan?
	✔ yes (attach) ___ no
What works/learns best when	**Other important information/ areas of concern**
Concrete, hands-on activities	
Communicate with both words and pictures	
Loves the computer!	
What does not work/ does not learn when	
Too much hovering by adults or kids	
Sudden changes in schedule, abrupt transitions	
Long drill-and-practice sessions of things she knows	

Figure 3.3. Student Information Form.

need a more comprehensive collection of biographical and educational information. A Student Notebook that includes additional information about the family, the student's IEP, instructional program plans, and evaluation tools is described in Chapter 4.

Program-at-a-Glance Although the classroom teacher and others who support the student need to be informed about the student's IEP, the IEP itself tends to be too cumbersome to be used for ongoing team planning regarding adaptations. The Program-at-a-Glance is a communication tool designed to give the classroom teacher and others who work with a student a quick overview of the student's educational program. Usually completed by the special education teacher, it includes a brief list of IEP objectives and accommodations. It also provides information about the student's academic or social management needs, including references to behavior management plans and feeding, positioning, or toileting needs. The Program-at-a-Glance can be provided on the back of the Student Information Form and copied on brightly colored paper for easy retrieval. Figure 3.4 shows a Program-at-a-Glance for Melanie.

Information About the Classroom

In order for the student to be meaningfully included, his or her team needs to know certain information about the classroom; it is important to understand the classroom's typical rhythms and routines, the way the teacher instructs, and the ways the students interact. Each classroom has its own unique structure and climate, both of which should be reflected in the student's plan for adaptations.

Program-at-a-Glance

Student _____ *Melanie* _____   **Date** __*10/96*__

IEP objectives	**IEP accommodations**
Social/communication	• *Receive special education assistance/ instruction with academics, daily routines, transitions, support for communication techniques, peer interactions*
• *Use devices/systems to express needs, feelings, ask questions, make choices, yes/no, greetings*	
• *Use gestures consistently*	• *Weekly curricular adaptations by special ed. and general ed. teachers*
• *Relate recent events in two- or three-word sentences*	• *Designated location in school for breaks*
Functional skills	• *Home/school communication log*
• *Follow task directions from cues*	• *Educational team familiar with and uses all augmentative communication methods*
• *School arrival, departure, lunch routines*	
• *School/classroom jobs*	• *Intervention plan to teach relaxation & self-calming*
Math	
• *Identify # 0–1,000*	
• *# line for less than, more than*	
• *Time to minute (face, digit)*	
Language arts	
• *Comprehension questions, novels*	
• *Computer journal writing*	
• *Read/write/spell functional words*	
• *Inventive spelling for class assigns*	
Content areas	
• *Key words/concepts for each unit*	

Academic/ social management needs	**Comments/special needs**
• *Peer planning at beginning of year and as needed*	• *Anecdotal records for IEP progress*
• *Reduced information per page*	• *Core team mtgs. weekly; whole team monthly*
• *Checklists & graphic organizers for time limits & beginnings/endings*	• *share autism info. with all team members/ relevant staff*

Figure 3.4.   Program-at-a-Glance for Melanie.

Assessment of Classroom Procedures To know when adaptations are required, the team needs to assess the classroom, including its structure, routines, types of instructional activities, curriculum, and climate. The extent and detail of information needed varies greatly, depending on the student's age and support needs. For students with mild disabilities who participate in the general education curriculum with only intermittent support, an informal, global appraisal of the students' abilities and the demands of the classroom is often adequate. That is, the team can easily identify significant discrepancies among the students' current capabilities and those required for full participation in the classroom. For example, Troy can easily comprehend sophisticated academic material that is read to him. However, he is not able to read the material fast enough to complete in-class reading assignments and requires more than the allotted time to complete homework that involves reading. A formal observation of Troy's performance in each of his academic classes is not necessary for his teachers to know that he will require some adaptations and accommodations in any course that requires more than two or three pages of reading per day.

Designing effective adaptations for students who have simplified or alternative curriculum objectives, however, will at times require gathering more detailed information about things such as typical instructional formats and procedures, types of in-class and homework assignments, testing formats and types of tests, and classroom rules and expectations. An Assessment of Classroom Procedures is conducted by the special education teacher through classroom observations and an interview with the classroom teacher during the first few weeks of the school year or semester. This information is used both to identify when adaptations are needed and to provide support personnel, including assistants and related service providers, with information about the classroom. As with other aspects of the adaptation process, this assessment is performed period by period for both middle schools and high schools. In elementary schools, the daily classroom schedule usually reflects activities for each subject area and is divided into morning and afternoon sections; therefore, the assessment and the development of adaptation plans would follow that formula.

Figure 3.5 is an Assessment of Classroom Procedures for Sam's ninth-grade World Geography class. In the first section, *Instructional Activities,* the two teachers have listed the typical instructional activities and frequently used student responses or tasks. In this class, the teacher uses both whole-class activities (e.g., lectures, discussions, films), small cooperative group projects, and independent activities (e.g., textbook reading and seatwork). In the Adaptations needed? section, the special education teacher has made notes that will be used for the next step of the process—determining whether Sam can perform the particular activity independently or whether adaptations are needed.

For students with more extensive support needs whose curricular objectives are significantly altered to include functional skills and/or embedded motor, social, and communication skills, the Assessment of Classroom Procedures will include more detailed descriptions of the steps of each type of instructional activity and will require actual observations of the student's classroom performance. This assessment involves a step-by-step listing of the typical steps and procedures for each class activity or routine. It also includes an assessment of the student's current participation in each step. Using this information, the team identifies the skills and the individualized adaptations needed to increase the student's participation.

For example, Figure 3.6 shows part of an Assessment of Classroom Procedures for the calendar math routine that is conducted daily in Daniel's classroom. Daniel's teachers first listed all the subjects scheduled across the day (e.g., reading, language arts, math, art, music, physical education) and the typical activities that were used within each subject area. For math, the typical activities included number games and worksheets, counting centers, and

Assessment of Classroom Procedures

Subject/Grade Level _World Geography/9th_   **Date** _9/96_

Student _Sam_   **Teacher** _Sailor_

Instructional Activities		
Typical activities	**Frequently used student responses/tasks**	**Adaptations needed?**
Whole class		
• _Lecture/discussion_	• _Take notes from board and overhead projector; raise hands to volunteer answers to questions (daily)_	_Yes_
• _Maps_	• _Locate places, describe/discuss geographic features (almost daily)_	_No_
• _Films_	• _Take notes, discuss (≈1x/week)_	_No_
• _Oral reading of text_	• _students volunteer to read (2–3x/week)_	_No_
Small groups		
• _Cooperative projects_	• _Research, writing reports in groups of 4 (1–2x/week)_	_Yes_
Independent		
• _Silent reading_	• _(1–2x/week)_	_Yes_
• _Seatwork_	• _Answer chapter questions, look up vocabulary words, map worksheets (2–3x/week)_	_Yes_

Homework (frequency and approximate duration)   **Adaptations?** _Yes_
- _Mon. through Thurs., 20–30 minutes; usually have a few minutes at end of period to start_

Textbooks, other frequently used materials   **Adaptations?** _No_
- _World Geography text; atlas, globe, wall maps_

General education teacher assistance   **Adaptations?** _Yes_
- _Teacher circulates throughout room, providing many opportunities to ask questions; checks frequently for understanding. Students are encouraged to ask questions of one another._

Evaluation/testing   **Adaptations?** _Yes_
                                                                             (As per IEP)
Test/quiz format
- _Unit tests: multiple choice, matching, true/false_
- _Vocabulary quiz for each unit: fill in the blank_

Sources of information for tests
- _Textbook, lecture notes, worksheets_
- _Review 1 day prior to test: good opportunity for students to prepare study guide_

Rules, norms, routines   **Adaptations?** _Yes_
                                                                             (As per IEP)
Classroom rules and contingencies
- _Must bring textbook, paper, pencil_
- _strict enforcement of school conduct code re: attendance, appearance, language, etc._
- _Students responsible for making up all missed work within 2 days of absence or no credit_

Norms for student interaction and movement (talking, moving around the room, etc.)
- _Raise hand during lecture/discussion; talking okay while working in groups_
- _May move around to sharpen pencils, get atlases, etc., except during lecture or test_

Procedures for routines (lining up, handing in assignments, assigned jobs, etc.)
- _Student at front of each row hands out/collects papers_
- _Folder on teacher's desk with previous day's handouts for students who are absent_

Figure 3.5. Assessment of classroom procedures. (Contributed by Johnna Elliott.)

Assessment of Classroom Procedures: Detailed Ecological Assessment

Teacher _____James_____ **Class/Grade** _1st_ **Student** _Daniel_
Subject _Math_ **Activity** _Calendar Math_ **Time** _12:15–12:35_ **Date** _9/12/96_

Typical sequence of steps/procedures	Target student participation
1. Teacher calls for attention; tells students to sit on floor in front of room.	1. Full physical assistance from assistant to walk to front and sit on floor; other students are seated and teacher has begun by the time D. is seated.
2. Teacher points to date chart; students respond orally as she asks for yesterday's date, today's date, number of days of school left yesterday and today, and is today's number bigger or smaller?	2. Assistant positions D. on floor and provides hip support. D. attends to teacher.
3. Teacher calls on one student to tell today's weather and makes tally mark beside the symbol; she asks for number of days we have had with that weather; students count tallies by 5s and then 1s.	3. Assistant cues Daniel: "Let's clap," when teacher asks students to count aloud. He claps assistant's hand as she counts aloud in Daniel's ear.
4. Teacher: "Yesterday was [names day of week]; today is [students say day of week]." Students and teacher spell day of week while clapping for each letter; then two to three students are called on to spell the day and clap independently.	4. Assistant cues Daniel: "Let's clap [number of letters in the day of the week]." Daniel claps her palm as she counts aloud in his ear then grasps his hand to signal "stop."
5. Teacher points to strings of beads labeled 100s, 10s, 1s; adds one more; calls on one student to count the beads, then another to say the number.	5. Daniel attends to teacher.
6. Teacher: "Let's count" [all count by 10s and 1s to day of the school year].	6. Daniel's head drops as assistant repositions herself.

Skills needed to increase participation

1. Raise hand to signal teacher for opportunity to respond
2. Count by 1s to 10 (by clapping another person's hand)
3. Answer yes/no questions using switch

Adaptations needed to increase participation

1. Get to front of room sooner—carry him or start sooner?
2. Yes/no switchplate

Figure 3.6. Assessment of classroom procedures: Detailed ecological assessment. (Contributed by Johnna Elliott.)

calendar math. As shown in Figure 3.6, Daniel's special education teacher observed the calendar math activity and wrote down a description of the typical sequence of steps and procedures, in addition to what Daniel actually did during each step and whether the assistant supported him at the time. Thus, for students such as Daniel, the Assessment of Classroom Procedures is similar to the ecological assessment process used to identify IEP objectives and adaptations in the community-living domains except that it is conducted in a classroom environment. (For more information on the ecological assessment process and using it to develop a community-referenced IEP, see Ford et al., 1989, and Giangreco, Cloninger, & Iverson, 1998.)

Step 2
Determine When
Adaptations Are Needed

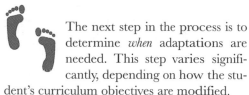 The next step in the process is to determine *when* adaptations are needed. This step varies significantly, depending on how the student's curriculum objectives are modified.

For Students with Simplified Curriculum

For students with simplified curriculum, adaptations can be developed directly from the Assessment of Classroom Procedures. That is, the teacher can simply note on the Assessment of Classroom Procedures whether each task or activity needs to be adapted. For example, as indicated on the assessment of Sam's World Geography class (see Figure 3.5), Sam needs adaptations during lectures and discussions, small-group cooperative projects, and seatwork; however, he can participate independently during map reading, watching films, and oral reading from the text. He also will need adaptations to homework and tests.

For Students with Altered Curriculum

If a student's curricular objectives are significantly different from those of his or her class-

mates, the student's adaptation plan must indicate how the student's objectives dovetail with those of other students. Curriculum matrixing is a process to accomplish this.

Program Planning Matrix When the curriculum is altered to include functional and/or embedded skills, another step is required to determine when adaptations are needed. First, the student's team must know when and where the student's altered objectives will be taught. The Program Planning Matrix helps them to analyze which altered curriculum objectives will be addressed in each class activity. The Program Planning Matrix is completed by the core team, with the guidance of the special education teacher, as early in the school year as possible. As shown in Figure 3.7, the student's IEP objectives are listed on the left-hand side, and the class activity schedule is listed across the top. An "x" in a cell indicates the IEP objectives that will be addressed during the corresponding class activities.

Melanie's IEP objectives include both simplified academic objectives as well as alternative objectives for functional skills and embedded social-communication skills. Matrixing is a straightforward process for the parts of Melanie's day during which her simplified academic objectives are addressed. Melanie's reading and writing objectives are addressed during the class journal writing activity, the language arts block, and the shared reading session while classmates are working on the same types of objectives. Melanie's alternative, functional skill objectives relating to her participation in school and classroom routines are also easily matrixed into the class schedule. She receives instruction and practice on her lunch, arrival, departure, and classroom job objectives at times when those activities are scheduled for the entire class.

However, Melanie also has several social and communication objectives (e.g., greeting and initiating interactions with teachers and peers, making choices, responding to yes/no questions). The benefit of matrixing is especially evident when identifying the most appropriate times to address these embedded

Program Planning Matrix

Student ___Melanie___   Class ___Ramirez/4th___   Date ___11/96___

Class Schedule (A.M.)

IEP OBJECTIVES	Arrival	Journal	Reading	Language skills	Break	Spelling	Math	Shared reading	Lunch
Communication									
Use pictures/devices to express needs, ask questions, initiate, make choices, yes/no	x	x	x	x	x	x	x		x
Relate recent events two- or three-word sentences		x	x	x					
Functional skills									
Use picture schedule to make transitions	x	x	x	x	x	x	x	x	x
Arrival/departure, lunchroom routines	x				x				x
Follow task directions from cues				x		x	x		
School/classroom jobs	x								
Math									
Identify # 0–1,000							x		
# line for ‹ , ›							x		
Time to minute (face, digit)							x		
Language arts									
Comprehension questions, novels			x	x					
Computer journal writing		x							
Read, write, spell functional vocabulary words		x		x	x				
Inventive spelling for class assignments		x		x	x				

Figure 3.7. Program planning matrix.

skill objectives. To be functional for Melanie, these social-communication objectives must be used within ongoing activities and routines. For example, using her communicator to greet and initiate interactions with other people is taught during times when it is natural for interactions to occur, such as during arrival, lunch, and recess. Besides indicating the most appropriate opportunities for addressing Melanie's social-communication objectives, the matrix also helps to ensure that *adequate* opportunities for instruction in those objectives are provided throughout the day. For example, Melanie's communication objective of using picture symbols and devices to answer yes/no questions is addressed not only during arrival, lunch, and break time, but also during journal writing, shared reading, and math. If she did not have repeated daily opportunities to use these augmentative communication systems, Melanie would be unlikely to become proficient in their use.

Another advantage of matrixing is that it allows the student's team to identify times for students to receive alternative services, such as direct service from a speech-language therapist, physical therapist, or vision specialist. For example, Daniel, our first-grade case study student, has an objective of using his walker for 20 minutes per day. Daniel was able to practice using his walker by moving about the classroom and by traveling with the class to the gym or library; however, his slow speed in using the walker made it difficult for him to keep up with his classmates. At the same time, Daniel's team had not been able to find meaningful ways for Daniel to participate in the second half of the "language skills" activity. Therefore, Daniel's classroom teacher would save errands for Daniel and a peer (who always completed her language skills activities quickly) to do at that time. Either the physical therapist or an instructional assistant would accompany the peer and Daniel as he used his walker for increasingly lengthy excursions throughout the school.

Once the IEP objectives for each scheduled activity or class are identified on the Program Planning Matrix, it is sometimes helpful to use the cells on the matrix for additional aspects of program planning. For example, the cells could be coded to indicate which type of adaptations are required for each activity by highlighting the cells that will require general adaptations in yellow and those that will require specific adaptations in green.

A thorough description of the use of the Program Planning Matrix as a tool to develop inclusive programming for students with severe disabilities is provided by Falvey (1995) and Giangreco et al. (1998).

Step 3
Strategies for Planning Adaptations

After the team has determined when adaptations are needed and whether they will be general or specific adaptations, the next step is to decide how and when the adaptations will be planned. The choice of adaptation planning strategies is affected by numerous factors, including the number and types of adaptations needed, the school level (i.e., elementary, middle, and high schools all present different planning challenges and advantages), teachers' schedules, the number of students with IEPs within the class, the availability of support personnel to provide in-class support, and the teachers' planning styles. The core team, especially the general and special education teachers, must decide on the ways that they will plan, communicate, and monitor the student's adaptations.

Figure 3.8, the Adaptations Planning Strategies Guide, is an example of a form that can be used to clarify and communicate the planning strategies agreed on by the core team. This guide is completed as soon as possible in the school year or semester and then later adjusted as necessary. It includes answers to questions such as, "When will we meet?", "How and when will we exchange materials that need to be adapted?", and "What happens if we run into problems?" The completed Adaptations Planning Strategies Guide shown in Figure 3.8 was developed for Sam who participates in a simplified academic curriculum. Similar to the other forms and processes described in this book, an Adaptations Planning Strategies Guide is typically prepared for each class at the secondary level and for the entire day at the elementary level.

Step 4
Plan and Implement General Adaptations

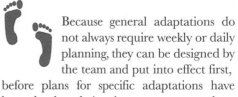

Because general adaptations do not always require weekly or daily planning, they can be designed by the team and put into effect first, before plans for specific adaptations have been developed. Another reason to put these adaptations in place first is that they establish the student's participation in the routines and ongoing activities of the classroom. Similar to

---

Adaptations Planning Strategies Guide

Student _____Sam_____ **Class** _World Geography/9th_ **Date** _10/96_

Classroom Teacher _____Sailor_____ **Special Education Teacher** _____Elliott_____

Meetings: **When?** _Thursdays after school_ **How Long?** _20 minutes_

Planning Format: _Elliott will prepare an Adaptations Plan describing the general adaptations for each type of class activity. The Adaptations Plan will also list which activities and materials will need specific adaptations. Elliott also will prepare a form for the Weekly Plan for Specific Adaptations._

How will objectives be adapted?: ✓ Simplified _____ Altered (functional/embedded skills)

Materials to be adapted:

✓ worksheets ✓ homework _____ textbook ✓ study guides ✓ quizzes/tests

✓ other: _Elliott will prepare five daily note sheets that include key word or concept for the day and targeted map symbols and geographic features._

Plan for exchanging materials that need to be adapted:

Tests/quizzes, study guides, and list of homework assignments that need to be adapted will be delivered at weekly planning conference. Special education teacher will drop off adapted materials and tests the day before they are to be used.

Default plan: What will we do if either of us defaults on our responsibilities?

Special education teacher: _Prepare folder of alternative activities to keep in classroom_

Classroom teacher: _"Punt" if doesn't deliver plans/materials to be adapted to special education teacher by Thursday_

Additional comments:

Figure 3.8. Adaptations planning strategies guide. (Created from ideas contributed by Johnna Elliott and Cynthia Pitonyak.)

all adaptations, they should be designed to be "only as special as necessary" in keeping with the hierarchy of adaptations described in Chapter 2.

Adaptation Plans for Students with Simplified Curriculum

For students such as Sam, who participate in a simplified curriculum, a one-page Adaptations Plan (Figure 3.9) can include most of the information needed to implement the student's general adaptations as well as notes about what specific adaptations will be planned each week. Sam's general adaptations focus on the ways in which in-class assistance with note taking, silent textbook reading, and individual seatwork will be provided for him and how tests will be adapted. For example, during lecture and discussion portions of the class, the instructional assistant will assist Sam in using the daily note sheet (prepared by his special education teacher) to record main ideas and key concepts. During the class review sessions on the

Adaptations Plan

Student _____Sam_____ Class __World Geography/9th__ Date __10/96__

Classroom Teacher __Sailor__ Special Education Teacher __Elliott__

Objectives: _1. Recognize and recall one main idea/concept per day._

2. Use and define selected terms related to geographic features, map symbols.

Class activity	General adaptations	Specific adaptations*
Lecture/ discussion	Assistant will assist Sam in using a daily note sheet to list main ideas, key concepts in his notebook.	Identify one main idea/concept per day.
Silent reading of text	Assistant or peer will read from the text with Sam.	Highlight main ideas/key terms in text.
Cooperative projects	Place Sam in group with peers who know him well.	Identify Sam's specific tasks and contributions.
Individual seatwork	Assist Sam with reading directions; provide prompts, as necessary, referring to necessary sources of information that should be used (text, notes, maps).	Adapt worksheets as necessary.
Tests/ quizzes	During class review session the day before the test, assist Sam in preparing his own study guide. Send Sam to Resource for tests; Elliott will assist with reading and recording answers, as per IEP accommodations.	Main ideas/concepts listed on sample study guide. All tests will be adapted.
Homework	Prompt Sam to record assignment in his blue notebook.	Simplify homework, reduce amount.
Alternative activities	If time is available because Sam has completed his work and does not have work from other classes to catch up on, he may go to the library for alternative activity (e.g., computer search related to chapter topic, current events in newspaper). Keep a record of times when alternative activities are used.	Generate ideas for specific alternative activities related to chapter topic.

Figure 3.9. Adaptations plan. (*Specific adaptations developed at weekly planning meeting.) (Contributed by Johnna Elliott.)

day before each test, Sam will receive assistance to prepare a study guide. For tests, Sam will leave the classroom, and the special education teacher will read the test to Sam—an accommodation that is listed on Sam's IEP.

Although the content of the specific adaptations designed for Sam will be planned weekly, the two teachers already have determined the types of activities and materials that will require weekly planning. Each week, the teachers will identify the daily main ideas or concepts that Sam will learn, adapt any worksheets as necessary, simplify and reduce the amount of homework given to Sam, and prepare sample study guides and adapted tests.

Classroom Participation Plans with General Adaptations for Students with Alternative Curriculum

In contrast to Sam's one-page Adaptations Plan, general adaptations for students with alternative curriculum objectives will typically be more extensive and will require use of a different, more detailed planning format. Classroom Participation Plans that include general adaptations to curriculum objectives, instructional procedures, and/or the classroom ecology are developed for these students. These plans, which are based on the student's IEP objectives and the classroom assessment information, are usually developed by special education staff, with input from the rest of the core team. The plans specify 1) the classroom schedule of activities, 2) the student's objectives for each activity, and 3) the general adaptations to procedures and materials that are used for instructing and/or supporting the student within that activity. Program plans for elementary students are developed for morning and afternoon sections of the daily schedule. For both middle and high school students, class-by-class planning formats may be more useful. These planning formats are tools for communicating program plans with classroom teachers and instructional assistants and can help to maintain the integrity of instructional programming for the student.

Figure 3.10 illustrates a Classroom Participation Plan with General Adaptations for Melanie. On Melanie's Classroom Participation Plan, the class subject or activity appears in the first column. Her IEP objectives for each activity (as determined by using the Program Planning Matrix) are listed in the second column. The third column describes the general adaptations and procedures that should be followed to instruct or support Melanie during each activity. However, Melanie's IEP also includes some simplified objectives in reading, math, and the content areas. Therefore, in the third column, the need for weekly planning of specific adaptations to these subject areas has also been noted. In addition, Melanie's plan reflects the ecological adaptations designed to help support her behavioral needs. The breaks scheduled into Melanie's day that provide her with the opportunity to move around and to calm herself are indicated in the General Adaptations and Procedures column.

ADDITIONAL OPTIONS: BEHAVIORAL SUPPORT PLANS

For students with significant behavioral needs, a Behavioral Support Plan is another format for planning general adaptations. A Behavioral Support Plan includes strategies for preventing problems from occurring and instructional strategies to teach the student alternative skills to replace the problem behavior. The plan should also include responding and/or crisis management strategies, which may involve strategies to protect the student, as well as others, during serious incidents. More information about supporting students with difficult behavior in inclusive environments is provided in *Behavioral Support* (Janney & Snell, 2000), another booklet in this series.

Step 5
Plan and Implement Specific Adaptations

 Once general adaptations are in place, planning and implementation of specific adaptations become a priority. Specific adaptations are designed for a particular lesson or activity and require weekly or daily planning. They include simplified curriculum content as well as instructional adaptations designed to match a specific lesson or activity (e.g., student materials, assessments, methods for teaching a particular skill or concept).

Weekly Plans for Specific Adaptations

Weekly planning is usually required for preparing specific adaptations, especially beginning in the intermediate grades and through high school as the curriculum becomes more complex and more paper-and-pencil tasks are required of students. The best possible scenario involves collaborative planning of lessons and activities by the special education and general education teachers. Not only does collaborative planning ensure that the two teachers have communicated about lesson plans and adaptations, it also promotes greater

Classroom Participation Plan with General Adaptations

Student _Melanie_   **Class** _Ramirez/4th_   **Date** _9/14/96_

Curricular Adaptations _Simplified and Alternative_

Activity	IEP objectives	General adaptations and procedures
9:00–9:10 Arrival	• Picture schedule • Greetings: "Hi, ___(name)___ "	• Flip to picture symbol: Classroom/backpack. (_Note:_ Begin each activity by having M. flip to appropriate symbol on picture schedule.) • Monitor putting away belongings: notebook in desk, lunchbox in cubby, backpack on hook. • Greet, socialize with peers.
9:10–9:30 Journal writing	• Relate recent events in two- or three-word sentences • Computer journal writing	• M. will tell aide or peer one thing that happened yesterday that she liked. Write it down; have her copy it on computer and then read it.
9:30–10:15 Reading: Oral reading and discussion of text book selection	• Read, write, spell functional vocabulary words • Comprehension questions, novels; yes/no questions • "wh" questions	• Select at least one vocabulary word per week from the lesson. Have M. point to and read the word. • Ask M. yes/no questions about some aspect of the daily selection. If she answers incorrectly, restate the question. Prompt correct response after two errors. • Following oral reading of text or worksheet material, teacher will ask M. "wh" questions that approximate those asked of other students (e.g., students are asked, "How did Anna relate to her new stepsister?" M. is asked, "Who is the sad girl in the story?"). • Weekly planning of specific adaptations to vocabulary words and comprehension questions
10:15–11:00 Language skills/spelling: Individual worksheets on targeted skills	• Inventive spelling/class assignments • Follow task directions from cues • Read, write, spell functional words	• Weekly planning of specific adaptations to skill worksheets, as necessary • Movement break at approximately 10:30
11:00–11:15 Shared reading	• Make choices, yes/no questions • Comprehension questions, novels	• _Materials:_ novel
11:15–12:00 Specials		
11:30–12:00 lunch	• Follow lunch routine with minimal prompting • Use communication devices to initiate, make choices	

Figure 3.10. Classroom Participation Plan with General Adaptations.

parity in their relationship, as both teachers become more responsible for the entire classroom group. Collaborative planning formats for specific adaptations typically include the daily schedule, the specific planned activities for each subject, and the necessary adaptations to those activities. In the beginning of the year, the special education and general education teachers can devise a planning format suited to the schedule and sequence of activities in that class. These forms can be stored on computer files so that necessary changes in the form can be made as the year progresses. Figure 3.11 illustrates the Weekly Plan for Specific Adaptations that was designed for Melanie.

Planning formats for middle or high school typically include only the adaptations designed for one particular class period. Figure 3.12 shows a planning format that is used each week to plan adaptations for Sam's ninth-grade World Geography class. The first column of the table lists the typically occurring activities that need specific adaptations (based on information from the *Assessment of Classroom Procedures*). For Sam, these activities include in-class text reading, lectures/discussions, individual written worksheets, and tests every Friday. The second column is used to note the specific adaptations that will be required to those activities for the week. For example, during lecture and discussion portions of the class, Sam completes daily note sheets prepared by the special education teacher. These note sheets will prompt Sam to record information about the main ideas or concepts that have been targeted as his daily objectives.

Step 6
Plan and Implement Alternative Activities

There are times when a team has not yet found a way to integrate a student's objectives into ongoing classroom activities or to effectively support a student within an existing activity. In such cases, alternative activities may need to be developed, at least until the team has had a chance to analyze the problem and develop additional ways to make the challenging activity more meaningful for the student with an IEP. For example, alternative activities might include the following:

- Community-based instruction in functional skill routines such as grocery shopping or restaurant use

- Intensive instruction in basic reading or math skills

- Opportunities to preview and review academic content

- Opportunities for intensive support in the development of motor skills

- Lists or folders of in-class activities related to current themes or topics

Although, for clarity, these activities are considered *alternatives* to general class activities, it is actually preferable to think of them as *supplements* to general class activities. That is, the intent is for alternative activities to occur in addition to partial participation in instructional activities that occur in the general class, not as a replacement for participation in general class activities. When alternative activities are thought to be necessary, they should be designed cautiously and carefully in keeping with the following guidelines. Alternative activities should be

1. Brief and timed so that if students leave the classroom, they come and go at logical breaks in the classroom schedule

2. Temporary or involving ad hoc groupings that include classmates without disabilities

3. Coordinated with general education content, themes, and methods so that the student is not isolated from the rest of the class

4. Designed to provide intensive instruction in crucial IEP objectives that the student would not otherwise receive

Chapter 5 provides descriptions of some alternative activities that the teachers who

Weekly Plan for Specific Adaptations

Student _Melanie_ **Teacher/Class** _Saunders 4th_ **Week of** _2/7/97_ **Unit Theme** _Colonial Times_

Subjects	Class objectives	Activities	Specific adaptations
Reading/ language arts	1. Vocabulary/comprehension: _Julie and the Wolves_ 2. Written language skills: review capitalization, punctuation 3. Spelling strategies: "ie" endings	1. Use story elements and vocabulary to write new ending 2. Writer's worksheets: diary entries of boys/girls in Colonial Times 3. Skill worksheets (attached)	1. Vocabulary dictionary: Julie, wolves, trap, snow, knife, boots 2. Colonial booklet: identify key concepts and pictures; make key vocabulary into full sentences, type on computer 3. Brainstorm "ie" words after given examples; make sentences using keyboard
Science/ health	Science: animals and habitats in southwest Virginia	1. Text pp. 23–29 2. Expert groups research and present on one animal	1. Use picture prompts for text reading 2. Key concept/vocabulary: habitat, forest, wolf cub, carnivorous 3. Group work: type draft on computer; contribute two facts
Math	Geometry: types of triangles	1. Text pp. 40–44; do problems on p. 44 2. Tangram puzzles	1. Count and write number of triangles in each category 2. Tangram puzzles with class; make tangram picture, glue down
Social skills/ class meeting	Preparation for Williamsburg field trip	Problem solving and role playing re: expectations, safety rules	Make social story including safety rules; make index cards for each site visited

Figure 3.11. Weekly Plan for Specific Adaptations (elementary).

Weekly Plan for Specific Adaptations (Secondary)

Student _____ *Sam* _____   **Plan for Week of** _____ *11/96* _____
Teacher _____ *sailor* _____   **Class** _____ *World Geography/9th* _____

Class activity	Specific adaptations
Lecture/discussion: *Chapters 21 & 22:* *The Middle East & North Africa*	Main ideas/concepts: (one/day, highlighted on daily note sheets) Monday *Land mass (as compared with United States)* Tuesday *Climate: desert* Wednesday *Water as main resource* Thursday *Three major world religions developed here* Friday *Conflict: Muslim vs. Judaism*
In-class text reading	Reading for the week: *Ch. 21—highlight key concepts*
Map reading: *political, physical, population*	Maps and symbols: *names of countries, settlements near water*
Films	Titles: *"The Wonder of Israel"*
Cooperative projects: *MAC Globe Project*	Collect information for the group on: *population, industry vs. agriculture, literacy & mortality rates. Create charts/graphs to display information.*
Individual written work	Chapter questions: *none* Worksheets: *Fill in the blanks on Venn diagram comparing and contrasting geographic elements; all students will work cooperatively, so no adaptations needed.*
Tests (every Friday)	Format for class review session on Thursday: *Small groups will prepare study guides; no adaptations needed; just provide occasional prompts to keep S. on track.*
Alternative activities	Ideas for alternative activities: Catch up on: *MAC Globe project* Library activities:

Figure 3.12. Weekly plan for specific adaptations (secondary). (Contributed by Johnna Elliott.)

contributed to this booklet have designed and implemented.

PUTTING THE STEPS TOGETHER

To provide an example of how the adaptation planning process looks when it is used to plan for an individual student, the steps that Daniel's core team took to plan for his year in first grade are described in the following paragraphs.

In June, during the week before school ended, Cyndi Pitonyak, the special education consulting teacher, shared Daniel's Student Information Form and Program-at-a-Glance with Ms. James, the first-grade teacher. Because Cyndi had already supported other students in Ms. James's classroom and was already familiar with the classroom routines, she and Ms. James already had completed the Assessment of Classroom Procedures. When school started in late August, Cyndi spent several days observing Daniel in the classroom to conduct a Detailed Ecological Assessment, which assessed Daniel's current level of participation and the need for supports and adaptations. During this time, Cyndi also drafted Daniel's Program Planning Matrix, tentatively identifying the classroom activities during which each of Daniel's IEP objectives would be addressed.

During the second week of school, Daniel's "core team," including Cyndi, Ms. James, Daniel's parents, the instructional assistant, and the physical therapist, met to brainstorm about adaptations for Daniel. The team discussed each classroom routine and activity to generate creative and educationally relevant ways to enhance Daniel's participation in the classroom. At the end of this meeting, Cyndi and Ms. James completed the Adaptation Planning Strategies Guide. They tentatively agreed to meet for 30 minutes each Thursday, while the students were participating in music class, to plan for the following week. Because Cyndi also provided consultative services for three other students in Ms. James's class, the two teachers would also use this planning time to collaboratively design activities to accommodate both Daniel and the other students with IEPs and to generate ideas for specific adaptations.

Throughout September, Cyndi observed Daniel in the classroom and drafted Classroom Participation Plans with General Adaptations for Daniel's participation in predictable class routines and activities. She reviewed these draft plans with Ms. James and the instructional assistant and modeled some of the teaching techniques that seemed to work best for Daniel. Until these Classroom Participation Plans were firmly in place, Cyndi and Ms. James did not hold their weekly meeting to plan specific adaptations. Instead, Cyndi checked in daily with Ms. James while the students were in art, music, or physical education class to learn about specific materials and activities that were planned for the following day.

The primary activities that required specific adaptations for Daniel were math and language arts. When Cyndi and Ms. James began holding weekly planning meetings during the last week of September, they discussed the specific adaptations needed for the following week. They also discussed any problems that had arisen and made any necessary adjustments to Daniel's instructional program plans and general adaptations.

Also during September, a team meeting that included the physical, occupational, and speech-language therapists was held. At this meeting, the team discussed ways to integrate Daniel's communication and motor skill needs into his classroom activities. The group scheduled in-class sessions with the vision teacher twice per week during language skills activities. Pull-in physical therapy was scheduled during physical education class, which provided a natural opportunity to overlap some of Daniel's motor objectives with those of his classmates. Occupational therapy sessions were scheduled twice per week during Learning Centers, during which Daniel could use his walker to move from one center to another and could handle the manipulative materials that were used for center activities. Cyndi also agreed to generate a list of supplementary unit activities (see Figure 5.2) to coordinate with each thematic unit completed by the class. These alternative activities would extend the unit into the tactile and kinesthetic modes that were so important for Daniel because of his visual impairment. Cyndi and the instructional assistant kept a record in Ms. James's class notebook of the times when these alternative activities were used because specific adaptations had not been designed in advance for Daniel.

Daniel's "full team," including his parents, Ms. James, Cyndi, the vision teacher, the occupational therapist, the physical therapist, and the instructional assistant, scheduled a meeting once every 6 weeks. At these meetings, the team reviewed Daniel's progress and evaluated the adaptations they had been using.

Chapter 4

Team Communication,
Monitoring, and Evaluation

This chapter briefly addresses some key issues related to how the core and extended teams will communicate about and evaluate adaptations and support plans. The companion booklet, *Collaborative Teaming* (Snell & Janney, 2000), goes into greater depth about these processes and discusses ways to organize and communicate about adaptation plans in classrooms in which several students with disabilities are supported by a team of general and special educators.

TEAM PROBLEM SOLVING ABOUT CHALLENGES

Designing adaptations, similar to teaching in general, requires ongoing evaluation and problem solving. This chapter provides a brief look at some processes and strategies that teams can use when new adaptations are needed or when existing adaptations need revision.

Ongoing Team Planning and Problem-Solving Meetings

Each student's core team will need to decide on a meeting schedule. In some cases, such as for core teams that serve students with extensive learning and support needs, a monthly planning and problem-solving meeting may be required. For students with less extensive needs, planning and problem-solving meetings may occur once each semester or grading period. These regularly scheduled meetings serve to review progress, revise general adaptations as necessary, conduct some creative problem solving regarding specific adaptations, and make plans to address any other issues or concerns team members might have. It is to everyone's advantage to make these meetings as efficient as possible. Some strategies to promote efficiency include assigning specific roles, firmly sticking to an agenda, and keeping strict time limits. Figure 4.1

Consultation Meeting Agenda and Minutes

Student _Melanie_   **Teacher/Grade** _Ramirez/4th_   **Date** _10/3/97_

People Present _Johnson (fourth-grade teacher), Pitonyak (IEP manager), Larsen_
(instructional assistant), Miotta (physical therapist)

Agenda Items/Decisions

1. _Classroom observations: Pitonyak to complete art and math this week._

2. _Food allergies: For now, cannot have ANY food not sent from home. Inform Mom of any_
   "slip-ups." Mom going to nutritional specialist next week and will give us more information.

3. _Communication: Pitonyak to complete communication demand log this week; will be kept_
   in notebook.

4. _Peer interactions: Alberts to take peer photos for communication book this week._

Next Meeting

Agenda Items: **Date:** _11/7_   **Time:** _8:00 a.m._ **Who:** _Full Team_

1. _Where to brush teeth_

2. _Schedule "messy" activities that require handwashing?_

3. _Times for therapists to be in classroom_

Figure 4.1.   Consultation meeting agenda and minutes. (Contributed by Cynthia Pitonyak.)

Student _____Sam_____   **Date** _9/29/96_

Team Members Present _Mr. and Mrs. X., Elliott, Sieff, Johnson, Learner, Sawyer_

Issue	Planned action	Who's responsible
1. *Sleeping in class*	1. *Go to bed earlier.* *Drink coke at lunch.*	1. *Parents* *Elliott*
2. *Interrupting others*	2. *Ask him to write down questions or remind him to wait.*	2. *All staff*
3. *Communication re: assignments, behavior*	3. *Write behavior notes in blue folder. Remind him to write assignments on Weekly Agenda forms.*	3. *All assistants*
4. *Inappropriate comments*	4. *"Let's get back on the topic." If continues, get a drink of water.*	4. *All staff*
5. *Other students who "push his buttons"*	5. *Help Sam to identify his behaviors that cause problems. Remind Sam to say to himself: "Get off my back" or "Grow up."*	5. *All assistants*

Figure 4.2.   Issue-Action Plan for Sam. (Contributed by Johnna Elliott.)

shows an example of a simple Consultation Meeting Agenda and Minutes form used at team meetings for Melanie. The team worked from a written agenda and strictly adhered to its 30-minute time schedule. Melanie's individualized education program (IEP) service coordinator took responsibility for taking minutes at team meetings and making copies of the minutes to distribute to each team member.

The Issue-Action Plan is another planning and problem-solving format that can be used at regularly scheduled or ad hoc team meetings to address adaptation challenges or other issues. (Chapter 1 describes the use of the issue-action format to address issues related to improving schoolwide inclusive practices.) Figure 4.2 is an Issue-Action Plan developed by ninth-grader Sam's team at an ad hoc team meeting that was called to address a number of concerns about his program, including Sam's reluctance to participate in class activities and the need to improve communication between Sam's teachers and his parents. The team began the meeting by list-

ing the issues they needed to discuss and then brainstormed possible actions to help address each issue. After selecting the best actions to take, the team assigned responsibilities to various team members. For example, to address the concern about Sam sleeping during class, his parents agreed to help Sam go to bed earlier, and the IEP service coordinator agreed to see that he drank a caffeinated beverage at lunch. Establishing accountability for the specific implementation responsibilities (actions) is aided by having the issue-action form printed on pressure-sensitive carbon paper so that at the end of the meeting each person can keep a copy. This helps to ensure that team members know exactly what actions they have agreed to implement.

MONITORING AND RECORD–KEEPING

The way in which staff members monitor programs and keep records about students' learning progress also changes when students with IEPs are included in general classrooms.

A number of teachers and assistants may instruct and support the student and, thus, may need access to information about the student's program. By developing ways to make this information accessible to various team members, it is important to guard confidentiality of these records at all times. Symbols or codes can be used to identify student records that are required for instructional purposes, or records can be identified using teachers' names rather than students' names.

Student or Classroom Notebooks

Large, three-ring binders are handy to use as planning and monitoring notebooks for students who require adaptations. Special education teachers who serve several or all of the students with IEPs in a given classroom may find it easiest to keep one notebook per classroom. Those who serve students across several classrooms may find individual student notebooks more helpful. The notebook provides a convenient vehicle for communication among team members. For each student, include the following information:

- Student Information Form (see Figure 3.3)
- Program-at-a-Glance (see Figure 3.4)
- Daily/weekly classroom schedule
- Related services schedule
- Assessment of Classroom Procedures (see Figures 3.5 and 3.6)
- Program Planning Matrix (see Figure 3.7)
- Data sheets and anecdotal records for monitoring IEP objectives
- Adaptations Planning Strategies Guide (see Figure 3.8)
- Adaptations Plan (see Figure 3.9) or Classroom Participation Plan with General Adaptations (see Figure 3.10)
- Weekly Plans for Specific Adaptations (see Figure 3.11 or 3.12)
- Lists of supplementary unit activities (see Figure 5.2)
- Tests and other written materials to be adapted

- Consultation Meeting Agenda and Minutes (see Figure 4.1) and Issue-Action Plan (see Figure 4.2)
- Home communication log
- Records of peer planning sessions
- Student work samples

Monitoring IEP Objectives

When the IEP service coordinator does not deliver all instruction to students with IEPs, it is important to have ways to monitor the implementation of instructional program plans. This is especially true when the special education teacher is an itinerant or consulting teacher and, thus, assistants provide much of the direct support for students with alternative curriculum objectives. The special education IEP service coordinator will want to develop a system for monitoring the implementation of instructional program plans, as well as for monitoring the student's learning progress. One strategy is to keep a log sheet in each student or classroom notebook on which teachers and assistants can record whether the student actually received the planned instruction. Brief forms used to gather feedback from classroom teachers about students' progress on their IEP objectives are also useful. A sample feedback form, which would be completed at the end of each grading period by the student's classroom teacher, is illustrated in Figure 4.3. On this form, the special education teacher has listed the IEP objectives for which feedback from the general education teacher is requested. For each objective, a rating scale from "seldom does this" to "consistently does this well" is provided. In this particular case, the special education teacher's concern was regarding the social and behavioral objectives of Andy, a student with a behavioral disorder. The feedback form was circulated not only to Andy's classroom teacher, but also to Andy's music, art, and physical education teachers. Although other, more objective and systematic evaluation of IEP objectives is important, it is also crucial to obtain informal feedback to help

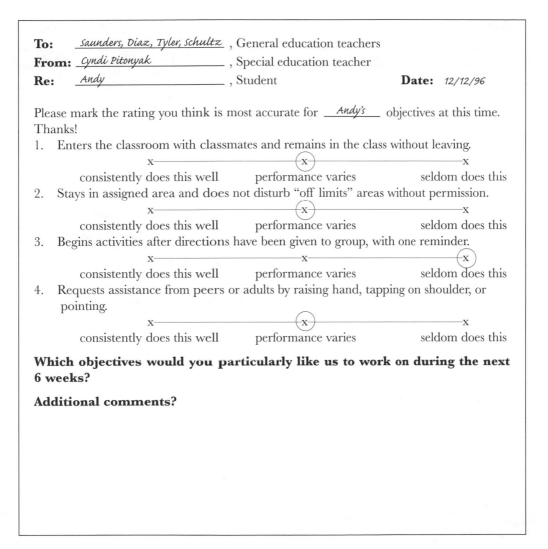

To: _Saunders, Diaz, Tyler, Schultz_ , General education teachers
From: _Cyndi Pitonyak_ , Special education teacher
Re: _Andy_ , Student   **Date:** 12/12/96

Please mark the rating you think is most accurate for _Andy's_ objectives at this time. Thanks!

1. Enters the classroom with classmates and remains in the class without leaving.

        consistently does this well   performance varies   seldom does this

2. Stays in assigned area and does not disturb "off limits" areas without permission.

        consistently does this well   performance varies   seldom does this

3. Begins activities after directions have been given to group, with one reminder.

        consistently does this well   performance varies   seldom does this

4. Requests assistance from peers or adults by raising hand, tapping on shoulder, or pointing.

        consistently does this well   performance varies   seldom does this

Which objectives would you particularly like us to work on during the next 6 weeks?

Additional comments?

Figure 4.3.   Feedback on IEP objectives from general education teachers. (Contributed by Cynthia Pitonyak.)

ensure that general educators are actively involved in evaluating students' progress.

Evaluating Team Functioning and Student Adaptations

It is important for teams to periodically evaluate both their functioning as a team and the quality of the work they are accomplishing. The most effective teams stop to ask one another, "How are we doing?" Student support teams also need to ask whether the adaptations and other modifications they have developed are helping students to participate actively in the classroom and to meet their learning goals while still being "only as special as necessary." Some sample questions that team members may want to ask themselves are provided in the Team Evaluation of Student Adaptations shown in Figure 4.4. Completing and discussing such an evaluation helps team members to ensure that the student is receiving quality inclusive programming and that the team members feel focused and effective working together.

Student _____ **Class** _____ **Date** _____

Team Member Completing Form _____

Yes	No	Criteria to meet regarding student adaptations
		1. I am clear about my role in designing and implementing adaptations.
		2. Decisions about adaptations are based on criteria that have been agreed on by the team.
		3. We have a system for solving problems related to the student's progress, behavior, and adaptations.
		4. The student receives adequate and appropriate in-class support.
		5. The student's curricular and instructional adaptations are "only as special as necessary."
		6. The adaptations enable the student to participate actively in class activities with peers.
		7. The student receives adequate instruction and practice in IEP goals/objectives.
		8. I am satisfied with the student's progress on IEP goals/objectives.
		9. The student's alternative activities are appropriate and do not prevent him or her from being a full member of the class.
		10. The student has a variety of positive relationships with peers.

Figure 4.4.   Team evaluation of student adaptations.

Chapter 5

Adapting Instructional Activities

This chapter provides some specific examples of ways to design and adapt instructional activities so that heterogeneous groups of students can participate together in shared learning experiences. Although the adaptations designed for each student must be individualized, it can be helpful to see or read about some of the adaptations that other teachers have devised for their students. Therefore, several lists of possible adaptations for some of the reading, writing, math, and testing activities encountered in inclusive classrooms are also provided.

DESIGNING INSTRUCTIONAL ACTIVITIES FOR STUDENTS WITH DIFFERING ABILITIES

In order to be fully included in the life of a classroom, students with individualized education programs (IEPs) must not be merely present; they must participate actively in social and academic activities with their classmates. This requires special education and general education teachers to collaborate to design units of instruction and daily lessons that are suitable for students with a wide range of interests, abilities, and learning styles.

Collaborative Planning of Instruction

General education classroom teachers, who are used to planning instruction for groups of students who participate in the standard grade-level curriculum, may be nervous about the idea of teaching students for whom this curriculum is not completely suitable. That is, including students with disabilities in general education classes requires rethinking the idea that all students in a class must learn the same things at the same time. Instead, what *is* important is that classmates share a common context for their learning experiences. Students can benefit, both academically and socially, from working together in shared activities, even if the objectives they accomplish within those activities are varied.

Multilevel Curriculum and Curriculum Overlap In an inclusive classroom, students'

individual curriculum objectives may differ in complexity or may be drawn from different subject or skill areas. Other researchers who have written about curricular adaptations have used the term *multilevel curriculum* to refer to lessons in which objectives with varying degrees of difficulty have been identified for various students. *Curriculum overlap* refers to lessons for which students' objectives are drawn from different subject or skill areas (Collicott, 1991; Giangreco & Putnam, 1991).

Chapter 3 examines the ways in which adaptations were planned for Melanie, the fourth-grader with simplified and altered (functional) curriculum objectives. During certain reading, writing, and math activities, Melanie worked on simplified versions of the class activity; however, at other times of day, the focus of Melanie's instruction was on functional skills, such as using a picture schedule, performing the cafeteria routine, or using her communication systems to make choices. Melanie's teachers used multilevel curriculum when they planned simplified reading, math, and content area objectives for Melanie but provided adaptations to ensure that she was engaged in activities with her classmates. For example, during writer's workshop sessions, Melanie participated in drafting and editing activities along with her classmates. Melanie, however, was completing sentence starters or story frames, whereas other students were generating their own topics and organizing their information. When Melanie's participation in a class activity focused on her functional communication, social, and motor skills, Melanie's teachers were using curriculum overlap while classmates worked on academic objectives. Thus, in social studies, Melanie worked with a cooperative group to make a model to illustrate their project on the shrinking habitat for black bears. Whereas the focus for classmates was on the social studies content that was used in making the model, the focus of Melanie's participation was on the motor and communication skills involved in constructing the model.

Both multilevel curriculum and curriculum overlap involve providing individualized adaptations to enable students with IEPs to participate in learning activities with their classmates. However, most teachers view multilevel instruction as "less special" than curriculum overlap. The "only as special as necessary" guideline urges teachers to establish multilevel objectives if such an adaptation leads to social and instructional participation for the student. If greater social and instructional participation can be achieved through curriculum overlap, then that type of curricular adaptation should be used.

Collaborative Planning of Instructional Units How do special and general education teachers work together to plan learning activities that use multilevel curriculum and curriculum overlap? "Up-front" collaborative planning of instructional units assists teachers in planning for the class as a whole, while still making provisions for individual differences. *Thematic units*, which integrate several curriculum areas under an organizing topic, are particularly well-suited to inclusive classrooms. An integrated curriculum provides a natural context from which students with differing interests and abilities can work toward curriculum objectives that vary in difficulty or come from various curriculum areas.

As indicated on the Unit Planning Format provided in Figure 5.1, collaborative planning of an instructional unit begins with identification of the "Big Ideas" (i.e., facts, terms, concepts, principles) as well as the skills or processes that are essential to the topic. These are the minimal competencies that are targeted for *all* students in the class. Thus, the more unique skills and content that particular students will need to learn in order to make the topic meaningful and useful to them are identified. These objectives include extended or advanced objectives for students who can go beyond those minimal competencies and simplified objectives for any students who need them. Next, the daily unit tasks and activities are listed, with an emphasis on designing activities that use as many input and output modes as possible. The major unit projects and activities are noted, along with notes about instructional adaptations that will be re-

quired for students with IEPs. This is also the time to designate the embedded motor, social, and communication skills that can be addressed within unit activities for students with more extensive disabilities.

Although collaborative planning of instructional units requires a significant initial investment of time, it makes adaptations more predictable in the future because many teachers use the same or similar units each year. If an entire grade-level team uses the same units, several teams' planning is assisted.

It may be useful to create a folder or list of alternative or supplementary activities for each thematic unit. These activities can be performed by any student but are especially helpful to have on hand during unit-related lessons that involve lengthy projects or activities that will require multiple adaptations for students with more extensive support needs. Figure 5.2 is a list of supplementary activities created for the Thanksgiving unit in Daniel's first-grade class. The advantage of this particular list is that it is organized according to the type of skill or ability—spatial, musical, body-kinesthetic, logical-mathematical, interpersonal, and intrapersonal—that is applied in each activity. Daniel's classroom teacher found that this list and others like it have provided her with many ideas for unit activities to do with the entire class.

Activity-Based Lessons

In addition to using the concepts of multilevel curriculum and curriculum overlap, providing instruction for mixed-ability groups is facilitated by the use of accommodating instructional arrangements, including activity-based lessons. Activity-based lessons are designed to provide instruction or practice within the context of an authentic, hands-on activity. This approach stands in contrast to lessons that use lectures, worksheets, and other more passive instructional formats to teach an isolated skill or concept. For example, the concept of equivalent liquid measures using cups, quarts, and gallons can be explained through a lecture and demonstration, following which students complete a worksheet that requires them to match

Unit Plan

Unit Theme: _____ **Teachers:** _____

Dates and Times: _____

Unit Goals: "Big Ideas" (Concepts, principles, and issues)	**Minimal Competencies**: (Essential facts, skills, and processes)
Extended/Advanced Objectives	**Adapted Objectives**

Tasks/Activities

____ Lecture _____

____ Reading _____

____ Discussion _____

____ Library research _____

____ Writing _____

____ Building/creating _____

____ Solving _____

_____

Major Unit Projects (Note adaptations)	**Supplementary Activities**
Evaluation Measures	**Adapted Evaluation Measures**
Materials Needed	**Adapted Materials Needed**

Figure 5.1.   Unit Plan.

Spatial (visual arts)
- Make placemats
- Make Pilgrim hats
- Pilgrim puzzles (clothing)
- Make November calendar
- Decorate bulletin board

Body-Kinesthetic
(performing movements)
- Thanksgiving finger play
- Dance
- Make sandwiches for dinner
- Pour drinks
- Pilgrim hat bean bag toss

Intrapersonal
(personal meaning)
- Family picture book
- Invite parents to "dinner"
- All decorations go home to be part of family Thanksgiving celebration

Musical
- Thanksgiving song (sing with class at start of unit activities)
- Play musical instruments
- Songs to go with clothing and food themes

Logical-Mathematical
(nonverbal problem solving)
- Set table: count plates, forks, cups, and so on
- Make cornucopia centerpiece with picture cues and numbers (e.g., five apples, two squash)

Interpersonal
(communicative/interactive)
- Match and write words with family pictures
- Thanksgiving symbol board
- Make "dinner" for peers and family

Figure 5.2. List of supplementary unit activities. (Contributed by Cynthia Pitonyak.)

pictures of equivalent amounts. The lecture and demonstration could be followed by an activity involving the use of liquid measuring devices to solve a series of equivalency problems, to make fruit juice from concentrate to serve to the class, or to fill the classroom aquarium using a number of equivalent measures.

Activity-based lessons are advantageous in inclusive classrooms for a number of reasons. First, hands-on, active learning is more beneficial than passive learning for many students. It not only gives practical meaning to otherwise abstract content but also assists students to construct knowledge through manipulation of interactive materials and primary data sources. Activity-based learning is particularly beneficial for students who need kinesthetic, tactile, or visual input.

A second advantage of activity-based lessons is that they provide a structure that makes it easier to address a variety of curriculum objectives within one lesson.

As part of a thematic unit on early American life, students in Mr. Ramirez's fourth- *grade classroom investigated the typical diets of the Native Americans and the early American Colonists. After studying the crops that were grown and the hunting practices used, the class prepared several foods using recipes that approximated those used in the late 1600s. One group of students—Melanie and three of her classmates—made corn bread. In designing the unit, Mr. Ramirez; the three other fourth-grade teachers; and Ms. Pitts, the special education teacher used Bloom's taxonomy of learning objectives to identify several levels of math and social studies objectives that could be addressed during each unit activity. For most students, the cooking activities were focused on math and social studies objectives at either the knowledge level or the application level. As shown in Figure 5.3, knowledge level math objectives included identifying the fractions used in the recipe and comparing the fractions used in the recipe by distinguishing whether the recipe required more shortening or more corn meal. At the next level of Bloom's taxon-*

Unit: Early American Life   **Activity: Making Corn Bread**
Multilevel Curriculum Objectives for Math
  Knowledge Level
    1. Identify the fractions used in the recipe.
    2. Identify relative size of whole and fractional parts: Does the recipe call for more sugar or more cornmeal? Which ingredient will you use least?
  Application Level
    1. Double the recipe. Express fractions in lowest terms.
    2. How many recipes will you need to make for each person in our class to have one 4″ × 4″ piece of cornbread? Multiply the recipe by that number.
Curriculum Overlap Objectives
  Motor Skills
    1. Pour milk into measuring cup without spilling.
    2. Stir batter using clockwise motion.
  Functional Reading and Math Skills
    1. Read the recipe.
    2. Measure ingredients with measuring cups and measuring spoons.
  Domestic Skills
    1. Get out and put away the ingredients.
    2. Wash dishes.

Figure 5.3.   Multilevel and curriculum overlap objectives for an activity-based lesson.

omy, application level *objectives included being able to double the recipe, expressing any of the fractions in lowest terms, and computing how many times the recipe would need to be multiplied for each person in the class to have one piece of cornbread.*

Mr. Ramirez and Ms. Pitts also identified objectives from the functional academic, domestic, and motor skill goal areas for certain students. Although many students in the fourth grade did not need instruction in skills such as reading the recipe and measuring ingredients using the correct measuring devices (e.g., a measuring cup for the milk, a teaspoon for the baking powder), the activity did provide a functional context within which to work on these functional reading and math objectives for other students. Motor skills, including pouring the milk and stirring the batter, as well as domestic skills, such as gathering and putting away the ingredients and cleaning up the cooking area, also provided instructional opportunities for some students.

During the baking activity, Melanie was able to complete the knowledge-level math objectives by responding to questions posed by Mr. Ramirez. Melanie also was able to practice her functional reading by being responsible for reading the recipe to her group. Melanie and another student in the class who has a physical disability also worked on motor skills targeted during the activity, which included pouring milk into the measuring cup and stirring the batter.

This is not to suggest that there is no place for skill-based instruction in an inclusive classroom. Students with and without IEPs often need direct instruction in specific skills and knowledge, along with adequate drill and practice in using those skills and knowledge. However, the end goal of learning is for students to be able to apply their skills and knowledge in a variety of meaningful contexts. Motivation, attention, retention, and generalization can be enhanced by providing instructional activities that allow students to apply skills from several domains in practical contexts.

Cooperative Learning

Both the philosophy and the structure of cooperative learning are well suited to inclusive classrooms. Cooperative learning teaches students to work together toward common goals and to value the range of contributions that can be made by individual group members. Johnson and Johnson (1991) described these five essential components of cooperative learning:

1. *Positive interdependence:* Group tasks are structured so that students need to rely on one another for the group to reach its goals. For example, each student fills a role in the group (e.g., facilitator, recorder, reporter, materials manager, "scout") and completes a particular part of the task. Teachers also can structure the task itself in ways that promote positive interdependence, such as by providing each group with only one set of materials.

2. *Individual accountability:* Although the group as a whole is responsible for achieving its goal, each member is also responsible for doing his or her part and for helping all group members to meet their learning objectives.

3. *Heterogeneous grouping:* Groupings typically maximize differences in ability and personal characteristics rather than minimize the range of skill or ability levels within the group. In many classrooms where cooperative learning is practiced not only do students belong to "base groups" with whom they work repeatedly, but they also may be grouped in a variety of other ways—by interest, gender, or prerequisite skills—depending on the nature of the specific activity.

4. *Direct instruction of social skills:* The social interaction and task-related skills required for the group to function effectively are actively taught by the teacher. Students are instructed in the use of effective communication and collaboration skills such as listening, encouraging one another, and negotiating conflicts. Teachers observe, evaluate, and provide feedback on the use of group skills.

5. *Group processing:* In addition to assessing how well they completed the task, groups are provided with structures to help them assess and improve their ability to communicate and work together. For example, at the end of the activity, each group might complete a self-evaluation instrument that includes questions about how well group members filled their roles and whether specified collaborative skills were performed.

Effective inclusive classrooms use both cooperative learning and peer cooperation as integral aspects of the classroom structure and culture. Cooperative learning will have little impact on students if it is practiced only during a few designated activities or if tasks are not structured to facilitate positive interdependence and students do not receive adequate instruction in the necessary skills to work cooperatively. A number of valuable references on cooperative learning are provided in the resource list in Appendix B, as well as in *Social Relationships and Peer Supports* (Snell & Janney, 2000).

ADAPTING READING AND WRITTEN LANGUAGE CLASSES AND ACTIVITIES

Supporting students who either do not read and write or who have very limited reading and writing abilities in classroom activities that place significant reading and writing demands on students can be a challenge. This section provides an array of suggestions for supporting students within some of the reading and written language activities that often are encountered in the upper elementary and secondary grades.

Adapting Literature-Based and Writing-Process Classes and Activities

With the increased use of literature-based and whole-language approaches to reading and the language arts, it becomes important to

1. Read the novel aloud to the student either one-to-one or in a small group. Frequently pose comprehension questions during reading.

2. The student, peers, or an adult can draw story strips or pictures as the story progresses. These materials can then serve as picture cues for discussing story grammar and the sequence and meaning of events in the story.

3. Create a picture dictionary of characters and important objects from the story (e.g., for *Julie of the Wolves*, include Julie, wolves, snow, knife, boots, and trap). The student can refer to the dictionary when answering questions or writing about the novel.

4. Create a story grammar booklet or a comprehension booklet with pictures. The pictures can be recreated from the book; drawn by adults, peers, or the student; cut from magazines; or printed from a computerized graphics program.

5. Create story grammar envelopes (i.e., characters, setting, problem, solution). Ask story grammar questions and then write the answers on cards. The student puts these in the appropriate envelopes and then can use the envelopes to create story webs, write chapter summaries, or review for tests.

6. Students who are not able to participate in writing activities can create products such as posters, dioramas, mobiles, paintings, and so on. The student presents the final product to the class using his or her own words or other communicative methods.

7. If it is believed that the student cannot effectively participate in a class novel, find other books on the same or similar topics and design a project that will relate to the class project.

Figure 5.4.   Ideas for adapting novel units. (Contributed by Kenna Colley.)

think of ways for students with limited reading and writing abilities to participate in ongoing classroom oral and written language activities. Although reading and writing can pose significant challenges even for students with relatively mild disabilities, creative planning and provision of appropriate accommodations and supports can ensure students' success.

Adapting Novel Units   Novel units are one approach to making reading and writing more interesting and meaningful for students. A *novel unit* typically includes a variety of listening, oral or silent reading, writing, and comprehension activities. Students are often given opportunities to choose the reading material and the methods they will use to study the novel. An array of suggestions for adapting novel unit activities is listed in Figure 5.4.

Adapting Literature Journals   Another typical ongoing activity in literature or literature-based classes is the literature journal. The literature journal is a tool for stimulating students to reflect on the literature they have selected and read. Students are typically given very general prompts to which they respond in their journal. This nondirected and unstruc-

tured activity can be impossible or nonproductive for students with limited reading or written language skills. The following is a list of suggestions for adapting literature journals:

1. *Provide stimulus questions.* Post a list of daily journal stimulus questions for the whole class or put a list of questions inside the front cover of individual students' journals. For a student who cannot face a blank page, structure the student's daily entry by writing the specific questions he or she is to answer that day. These questions can be selected in collaboration with the student in a brief interview. Here are a few examples of stimulus questions and adapted questions written at a lower readability level:

    *   *Stimulus Question:* Which character did you empathize with most? Why?
        Adapted Question: What person in the story did you like the best?
    *   *Stimulus Question:* What was the most significant aspect of the story you read today? Reflect on why you selected that aspect.

Adapted Question: What was the best part of the story you read today?

- *Stimulus Question:* What emotions did you experience while reading today? Reflect on the specific elements of the story that evoked those emotions.
  Adapted Question: How did you feel while reading today? Sad? Happy?

2. *Provide a scribe.* Pair a student who has difficulty with independent writing with another student. Both students read the same selection and collaborate on one journal, with the more competent writer scribing for the pair.

3. *Provide writing frames.* Students who need support with basic comprehension and writing can participate in literature journals if provided with a structured journal page that focuses on one or more elements of story grammar. For example, after the daily reading session, the student might name the main character, setting, and what happened. A teacher, assistant, or peer writes the responses on a card, and the student copies the information onto the journal page under the correct heading. Alternatively, the student might select one or more character, setting, or plot frames for

each daily journal entry, such as those illustrated in Figure 5.5.

ADAPTING LISTENING, READING, AND WRITING DEMANDS IN THE CONTENT AREAS

Students who have disabilities that affect their reading and writing skills can still gain much knowledge from the information provided in content area activities and classes. There are many ways that teachers can adapt the listening, reading, and writing demands that are placed on students in social studies, science, and health classes so that students can learn content objectives in spite of their difficulties with reading and writing. The following are ideas for making content area classes, especially those at the secondary level, more accommodating for students.

Adapting Lectures

Lectures can be adapted both by altering the input, or delivery, of the material and by adapting the output, or the response, required of the students. That is, teachers can assist students by adapting the format and delivery

---

Literature Journal

Date: _____   Last page number: _____

Book: _____

Author: _____

Why did you pick this book? _____

Who is in this story so far? _____

What is the main thing that happened in the story today? _____

Story Grammar Frame

Book _____   Chapter _____

Main Characters _____   _____

_____   _____

Where?_____

What happened? _____

Figure 5.5.   Structured literature journal pages. (Contributed by Christine Burton.)

Slot Notes

Class _____ Unit _____ Date _____ Name _____

I.   How do you get the flu?
    A. _____ virus invades the same tissues as _____ viruses do.
    B. Flu _____ are similar to those of a cold but more _____ .
    C. Treat it as you would a _____ ; rest.
    D. Flu spreads _____ : Epidemics may occur.
II. What causes pneumonia?
    A. _____ is an inflammation of the lungs.
    B. It starts by _____ or _____ growing in the _____ and _____ and moves to the _____ .

Figure 5.6.   Slot notes. (Contributed by Christine Burton and Johnna Elliott.)

of their lectures and the requirements for listening and note taking.

*Adapt the input
or instructional stimulus*

- Use a guided lecture procedure: review objectives, purpose, and relevance of the material; pause frequently; pose questions; summarize.

- Use a multisensory approach, including demonstrations, drama, music, and pictures.

- Use visual aids (e.g., advance organizers, semantic maps, outlines) to illustrate topics and subtopics and how they are related.

- Use temporal cues (first, next, last).

- Use controlled vocabulary; omit extraneous detail.

- Provide audiocassette recordings that students can listen to at home so that they can check or complete their notes.

Adapt the output or student response

- Provide slot notes (Figure 5.6): The teacher's lecture notes are printed or typed, leaving blanks or slots for the student to fill in during the lecture. Photocopies of the slot notes are made for any students who need them. An overhead transparency of the notes also can be made for the teacher to use to fill in the blanks as he or she lectures.

- Provide peer note takers.

Adapting Textbook Reading

Much of the support provided in inclusive middle and high school classrooms involves supporting students in meeting the reading demands of the class. Poor or nonreaders need adaptations and accommodations that will enable them to get the needed information from their textbooks in spite of their difficulties with reading. In middle and high school, it becomes imperative to assess the reading demands in each class in which a student with reading difficulties is enrolled. It can be useful to develop a support plan for each student who is taking content area courses but needs assistance with the reading demands of the class. As shown in Figure 5.7, a Plan for Reading Adaptations and Accommodations summarizes the reading task demands for each subject. It then lists the general adaptations and accommodations that will be necessary for each class and delineates which teacher or assistant is responsible for providing the identified supports. The special education teacher develops this plan and shares it with the classroom teacher and any instructional assistants that support students in the relevant classes.

Possible adaptations and accommodations to assist students with their textbook reading include adaptations to the instructional stimulus or input (i.e., changing the text's difficulty, amount, or format) and adaptations to the student response or output (i.e., changing the type of reading demand required of the

Plan for Reading Adaptations and Accommodations for: ___Mary___

Subject	Reading task demand	Adaptations and accommodations	Staff
English	Silent reading of novel 20 minutes/day; novels are two grade levels above her independent level.	• Silent/oral reading group option, selected by student preference • Day readers/night readers option	Teacher/ assistant/ peer
Math	Read and follow written directions on workbook pages and worksheets.	• Worksheets: Pair symbols with direction words; rewrite directions at lower readability. • Sight word drill of direction words, two 10-minute sessions/week	Special education teacher
Science	Follow oral reading of text by classmates and teacher; identify key vocabulary; learn definitions of key vocabulary for test.	• Teacher will not call on Mary to read aloud. • Highlight textbook: yellow = vocabulary word, blue = definition. • Notebook: Reduce note-taking requirement to copying highlighted vocabulary words and definitions. • Tests: two study sessions prior to test; read word, find definition.	Teacher Assistant special education teacher Special education teacher

Figure 5.7.   Plan for Reading Adaptations and Accommodations. (Contributed by Christine Burton.)

student). Some possible adaptations and accommodations for textbook reading include the following:

Change the instructional stimulus

• Rewrite short passages, or textbook directions, at lower readability.

• Have the student listen and retell, or read and retell, what he or she read.

• Add pictures or symbols.

• Provide multiple texts (or novels).

• Provide page and paragraph markers with simplified questions.

• Reduce text information to a study guide of concepts and vocabulary.

• Read only highlighted key concepts and vocabulary.

• Provide supplements such as tapes and films.

Change the output or student response

• Conduct paired reading sessions.

• Allow the option of silent or oral reading groups.

• Allow the option of reading at school during the day or at home at night.

ADAPTING MATH

The following is a list of some possible ways to adapt math instruction and activities:

• Provide and teach students to use manipulatives and/or pictorial representations of concepts and processes.

- Provide posters with words that indicate operations in word problems (e.g., words that mean addition, such as plus, more, more than, add, increase).

- Add cues to computational signs in texts and worksheets: " + means add", "– means subtract," or use color coding.

- Box computation items for students.

- Fold worksheets so students can work on one row at a time.

- Allow use of a calculator, number line, or multiplication table.

- Highlight directions and cues.

- On worksheets, reduce the number of items per page.

- Have the student complete fewer items (e.g., only every other item).

- Use large-print materials.

- Provide an example on worksheets and tests.

- Provide answer boxes.

- Establish motivation and relevance: Work real problems, conduct investigations.

- Use the following instructional sequence: 1) concrete, 2) pictorial or graphic, 3) abstract/symbolic.

- Use the following instructional sequence: 1) demonstration, 2) guided practice, 3) independent practice.

- Provide self-instructional training: Teach students to say the steps to themselves as they work a computation.

ADAPTING TESTS AND TESTING PROCEDURES

For many students with IEPs, accommodations to tests and testing procedures are the major accommodations on their IEPs. The issue in adapting testing is to carefully compare the student's objectives with what is being measured by the test and to avoid "testing" the student's disability. That is, if a student has a specific learning disability in written language and the objective of a social studies test is to evaluate the student's knowledge of academic content, then a timed essay exam may not be the best way to determine if the student has met the content objectives.

Another way to help ensure that students' learning is accurately represented by their test results is to teach test-taking skills. For example, you can explain, demonstrate, and have students practice strategies for taking multiple-choice tests. They should read all answers before selecting the best one, eliminate obviously incorrect choices, attempt all items, and do easier items first and then come back to items about which they are unsure. Strategies for taking essay tests include beginning with an outline or semantic map and planning how to allot time between drafting and revising.

Both testing procedures and the actual test formats used can be adapted to ensure that students' learning is fairly evaluated by a test. An array of examples follows:

- Use large print, and allow ample space between items.

- When constructing multiple-choice tests, list the choices vertically rather than horizontally under the stem.

- Provide a word bank for fill-in-the-blank items.

- For matching items, keep all matching items and choices on the same page.

- Rewrite directions at a lower readability level.

- Highlight important words in the directions and/or in test items.

- Read the directions aloud to the class and ask students to repeat the directions.

- Provide an example for each type of test item.

- Allow students to use aids, such as a calculator, manipulatives, or charts.

- Provide a scribe for the student; the student may or may not recopy the material.

- Allow a student to prepare a chart or map instead of writing an essay.

- Construct a Bloom's taxonomy essay test. That is, write test items to fit several levels of Bloom's taxonomy of learning objectives. Differentiate the point value of the items at the various levels (e.g., knowledge items are worth 5 points each, application items are worth 10 points each, and analysis or synthesis items are worth 20 points each). Students may choose items to equal 100 points as long as they choose from at least two levels.

- Provide alternative ways to demonstrate achievement: projects, surveys, maps, and oral reports.

ALTERNATIVE ACTIVITIES

There are a number of situations in which you may need to provide alternative activities for students. For example, a lengthy lecture or a prolonged period of independent seatwork can often be difficult to adapt for some students. It can also be difficult to design adaptations that will engage a student with significant support needs for the full duration of an extended activity, such as during a writer's workshop or block-scheduled middle or high school classes. In some cases, alternative activities may be required temporarily because ways to meaningfully address a student's alternative functional skill objectives within ongoing class activities have not been determined. At times, alternative activities may be needed because of unforeseen circumstances (e.g., when a teacher or assistant is absent and the planned adaptation is too complex for a substitute to implement, an assembly runs overtime and plans must be changed on the spot, a planned adaptation turns out to be a disaster).

The following section briefly examines several types of alternative activities and provides some guidelines for making them as unintrusive as possible.

Brief, Focused Instruction in Alternative (Functional) Curriculum Objectives

Alternative activities may be needed when a student's Program Planning Matrix indicates that the student's functional or embedded skill objectives have not fit well into classroom activities and, therefore, have not been addressed adequately across the day. The Program Planning Matrix can help to identify times when such instruction can occur without depriving the student of other important instructional opportunities. For example, Daniel was not receiving adequate amounts of time using his gait trainer (walker). Therefore, Daniel's team targeted several brief times during the day that provided logical opportunities for the physical therapist or assistant to help Daniel use his gait trainer without missing other needed instruction.

Ad Hoc Groupings of Students with and without Disabilities for Review or Corrective Lessons

Ad hoc groupings avoid identifying particular students as being always in need of extraordinary assistance. Instead of identifying permanent "remedial" groups, students can be identified for "pull-out" review or corrective sessions based on their need for specific prerequisite skills required to participate in class instruction. For example, one special education consulting teacher developed a writing laboratory as an alternative activity for a second-grade class that included Joel, a student with mental retardation. Three times per week, Joel and a small group of classmates went to the consulting teachers' office for a writing laboratory, while other students in the class were engaged in their writer's workshop activities. The students who participated in the writing laboratory with Joel were selected by the general education teacher based on her evaluations of the previous week's writer's workshop activities. In the writing laboratory, the special education teacher provided Joel and his classmates with small-group and individualized instruction that focused on the specific written language skills with which they were having difficulty.

Study Hall as a Resource Room

Middle or high school students can receive services, such as tutorial assistance with their content area classes or remedial assistance with basic reading, writing, or math skills, in

What the Research Says

Pugach and Wesson interviewed students with and without learning disabilities in two fifth-grade classrooms that were taught by a general education and a special education teacher. The special education teacher often provided instruction to small groups of three or four students. To avoid a group being viewed as "permanently skill deficient," groups were determined weekly and included any student who needed work on specific skills or concepts, especially in spelling and math. "Students [with learning disabilities] did not see their being taken out of the regular classroom for assistance on an ad hoc basis as problematic, in contrast to these students' dislike of formal, permanently established groups that met in resource rooms in prior years" (1995, p. 279).

Figure 5.8   Students' views of pull-out services.

a study hall attended by students with and without IEPs. In these study halls, which are staffed by general education and special education teachers and assistants, students with IEPs have the opportunity to receive additional support in their school work within a generic support setting rather than in a special education resource room, which high school students sometimes find stigmatizing (Figure 5.8).

Community-Based Instruction

According to the adaptations model, community-based instruction is considered to be an alternative instructional activity (unless it is conducted as part of the general education course offerings in the school). Community-based instruction was originally conceived as an important element of a functional, community-referenced curriculum. Its purpose is to teach "real-life" skills and activities in the environments where those skills ultimately are used. In inclusive elementary schools, community-based instruction is seldom scheduled solely for students with IEPs. Instead, special education students receive support to participate in field trips and other community experiences with their classmates, whereas the focus of their IEPs is on maximizing their participation in ongoing school and classroom activities. However, in inclusive middle and high schools, some students may receive instruction outside of school. The decision to provide out-of-school learning opportunities for students with IEPs is based on the student's and family's long-term goals and on the probability that

the student will require longitudinal planning and preparation for adult life in the community. After the age of 18 years, when their peers without disabilities are no longer attending high school, students with IEPs spend increasing amounts of time in job settings as they near graduation.

Lists or Folders of Alternative In-Class Activities

For times when a class activity lasts too long for a student to participate effectively, lists or folders of alternative in-class activities can provide suggestions for keeping the student in the classroom and engaged in activities related to the class subject area. For example, if engaging the student during the entire 75-minute block set aside for writer's workshop is a challenge, then the list can emphasize language arts activities (Figure 5.9). Or, if tenth-grade biology laboratory projects are the challenge, the list might provide ideas for using library books, computer games, videotapes, and posters to study the unit topic. Such alternative activities need to vary according to the content of class activities. That is, the specific activities listed need to change from time to time, as the class begins new projects or themes. However, the types of activities included will generally be somewhat consistent.

These subject area or thematic lists of alternative activities may also be used during "emergencies" or other unforeseen circumstances. Many classroom teachers have learning centers, folders of extension activities, or

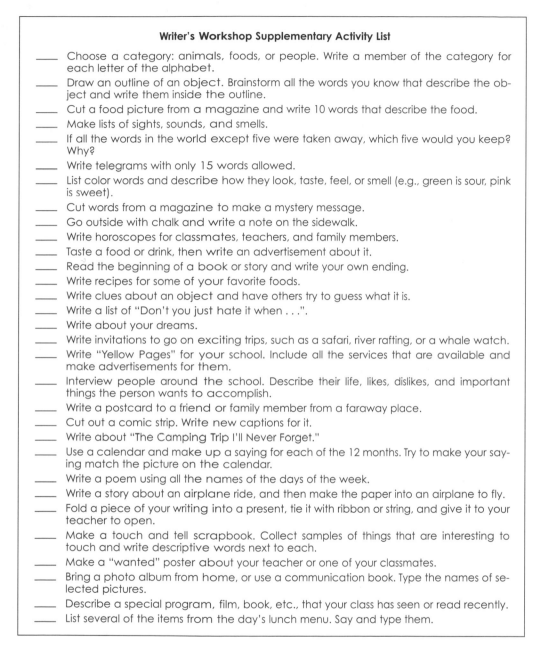

Writer's Workshop Supplementary Activity List

___ Choose a category: animals, foods, or people. Write a member of the category for each letter of the alphabet.

___ Draw an outline of an object. Brainstorm all the words you know that describe the object and write them inside the outline.

___ Cut a food picture from a magazine and write 10 words that describe the food.

___ Make lists of sights, sounds, and smells.

___ If all the words in the world except five were taken away, which five would you keep? Why?

___ Write telegrams with only 15 words allowed.

___ List color words and describe how they look, taste, feel, or smell (e.g., green is sour, pink is sweet).

___ Cut words from a magazine to make a mystery message.

___ Go outside with chalk and write a note on the sidewalk.

___ Write horoscopes for classmates, teachers, and family members.

___ Taste a food or drink, then write an advertisement about it.

___ Read the beginning of a book or story and write your own ending.

___ Write recipes for some of your favorite foods.

___ Write clues about an object and have others try to guess what it is.

___ Write a list of "Don't you just hate it when . . .".

___ Write about your dreams.

___ Write invitations to go on exciting trips, such as a safari, river rafting, or a whale watch.

___ Write "Yellow Pages" for your school. Include all the services that are available and make advertisements for them.

___ Interview people around the school. Describe their life, likes, dislikes, and important things the person wants to accomplish.

___ Write a postcard to a friend or family member from a faraway place.

___ Cut out a comic strip. Write new captions for it.

___ Write about "The Camping Trip I'll Never Forget."

___ Use a calendar and make up a saying for each of the 12 months. Try to make your saying match the picture on the calendar.

___ Write a poem using all the names of the days of the week.

___ Write a story about an airplane ride, and then make the paper into an airplane to fly.

___ Fold a piece of your writing into a present, tie it with ribbon or string, and give it to your teacher to open.

___ Make a touch and tell scrapbook. Collect samples of things that are interesting to touch and write descriptive words next to each.

___ Make a "wanted" poster about your teacher or one of your classmates.

___ Bring a photo album from home, or use a communication book. Type the names of selected pictures.

___ Describe a special program, film, book, etc., that your class has seen or read recently.

___ List several of the items from the day's lunch menu. Say and type them.

Figure 5.9. Writer's workshop supplementary activity list. (Contributed by Kenna Colley.)

other ways to provide students with supplementary activities to work on when they have extra time. Activities that would be appropriate for a student with an IEP can be included with these existing supplementary activity options.

It is helpful to monitor the use of alternative activities. One way to do this is to include a sheet in the student's record-keeping notebook on which he or she can jot down the times when these alternative activities were used. This enables the team to do some problem solving about the times when it was difficult to include the student in ongoing class activities so that the teacher can be more proactive the next time a similar activity occurs.

References

Baumgart, D., Brown, L., Pumpian, I., Nisbet, J., Ford, A., Sweet, M., Messina, R., & Schroeder, J. (1982). Principle of partial participation and individualized adaptations for severely handicapped students. *Journal of The Association for Persons with Severe Handicaps, 7,* 17–27.

Bloom, B. (1976). *Taxonomy of educational objectives.* New York: Longman.

Collicott, J. (1991). Implementing multi-level instruction: Strategies for classroom teachers. In G.L. Porter & D. Richler (Eds.), *Changing Canadian schools* (pp. 191–218). North York, Ontario, Canada: The Roeher Institute.

Davern, L., Ford, A., Erwin, E., Schnorr, R., & Rogan, P. (1993). *Working toward inclusive schools: Guidelines for developing a building-based process to create change.* [Special monograph] Syracuse, NY: Syracuse University Projects/Consortium. (Available from Huntington Hall, 150 Marshall Street, Syracuse University, Syracuse, NY 13244-2340).

Falvey, M.A. (1995). *Inclusive and heterogeneous schooling: Assessment, curriculum, and instruction.* Baltimore: Paul H. Brookes Publishing Co.

Ford, A., Messenheimer-Young, T., Toshner, J., Fitzgerald, M.A., Dyer, C., Glodoski, J., & Laveck, J. (1995, July). *A team planning packet for inclusive education.* Milwaukee: Wisconsin School Inclusion Project.

Ford, A., Schnorr, R., Davern, L., Meyer, L., Black, J., & Dempsey, P. (Eds.). (1989). *The Syracuse community-referenced curriculum guide.* Baltimore: Paul H. Brookes Publishing Co.

Forest, M., & Lusthaus, E. (1990). Everyone belongs with the MAPs action planning system. *Teaching Exceptional Children, 22*(2), 32–35.

Giangreco, M.F., Cloninger, C.J., & Iverson, V.S. (1998). *Choosing options and accommodations for children (COACH): A guide to planning inclusive education* (2nd ed.). Baltimore: Paul H. Brookes Publishing Co.

Giangreco, M.F., & Putnam, J.W. (1991). Supporting the education of students with severe disabilities in regular education environments. In L.H. Meyer, C.A. Peck, & L. Brown (Eds.), *Critical issues in the lives of people with severe disabilities*

(pp. 245–270). Baltimore: Paul H. Brookes Publishing Co.

Good, T.L., & Brophy, J.E. (1991). *Looking in classrooms.* New York: HarperCollins.

Janney, R.E., & Snell, M.E. (1997). How teachers use peer interactions to include students with moderate and severe disabilities in elementary general education classes. *Journal of The Association for Persons with Severe Handicaps, 21,* 72–80.

Janney, R.E., & Snell, M.E. (1999). *Teachers' guides to inclusive practices: Behavioral support in inclusive schools.* Baltimore: Paul H. Brookes Publishing Co.

Johnson, D.W., & Johnson, R. (1991). *Learning together and alone: Cooperation, competition, and individualization* (3rd ed.). Englewood Cliffs, NJ: Prentice-Hall.

Mount, B., & Zwernik, K. (1989). *It's never too early, it's never too late: A booklet about Personal Futures Planning.* St. Paul: Minnesota Governor's Planning Council on Developmental Disabilities. (Report No. 421-109).

Mount, B., & Zwernik, K. (1990). *Making futures happen: A manual for facilitators of Personal Futures Planning.* St. Paul: Minnesota Governor's Council on Developmental Disabilities. (Publication No. 421-90-036).

O'Brien, J. (1987). A guide to life-style planning: Using the Activities Catalog to integrate services and natural support systems. In B. Wilcox & G.T. Bellamy (Eds.), *A comprehensive guide to the Activities Catalog: An alternative curriculum for youth and adults with severe disabilities* (pp. 175–189). Baltimore: Paul H. Brookes Publishing Co.

Peterson, M., LeRoy, B., Field, S., & Wood, P. (1992). Community-referenced learning in inclusive schools. In S. Stainback & W. Stainback (Eds.), *Curriculum considerations in inclusive classrooms* (pp. 207–227). Baltimore: Paul H. Brookes Publishing Co.

Potter, M.L. (1992). Research on teacher thinking: Implications for mainstreaming students with multiple handicaps. *Journal of Developmental and Physical Disabilities, 4*(2), 115–127.

Pugach, M.C., & Wesson, C.L. (1995). Teachers' and students' views of team teaching of general education and learning-disabled students in two fifth-grade classes. *The Elementary School Journal, 95*(3), 279–295.

Putnam, J.W. (Ed.). (1993). *Cooperative learning and strategies for inclusion: Celebrating diversity in the classroom.* Baltimore: Paul H. Brookes Publishing Co.

Rainforth, B., York, J., & Macdonald, C. (1992). *Collaborative teams for students with severe disabilities.* Baltimore: Paul H. Brookes Publishing Co.

Schnorr, R.F. (1990). "Peter? He comes and goes . . .": First graders' perspectives on a part-time mainstream student. *Journal of The Association for Person with Severe Handicaps, 15*(4), 231–240.

Snell, M.E., & Janney, R.E. (2000). *Teachers' guides to inclusive practices: Collaborative teaming.* Baltimore: Paul H. Brookes Publishing Co.

Snell, M.E., & Janney, R.E. (2000). *Teachers' guides to inclusive practices: Social relationships and peer supports in inclusive schools.* Baltimore: Paul H. Brookes Publishing Co.

Strickland, B.B., & Turnbull, A.P. (1990). *Developing and implementing individualized education programs* (3rd ed.). Columbus, OH: Merrill.

Thousand, J.S., Fox, T.J., Reid, R., Godel, J., Williams, W., & Fox, W.L. (1986). *The Homecoming Model: Educating students who present intensive educational challenges within regular education environments.* Burlington: University of Vermont, Center for Developmental Disabilities.

Thousand, J.S., Villa, R., & Nevin, A.I. (Eds.). (1994). *Creativity and collaborative learning.* Baltimore: Paul H. Brookes Publishing Co.

Udvari-Solner, A. (1994). A decision-making model for curricular adaptations in cooperative groups. In J.S. Thousand, R. Villa, & A.I. Nevins (Eds.), *Creativity and cooperative learning* (pp. 59–77). Baltimore: Paul H. Brookes Publishing Co.

Vandercook, T., York, J., & Forest, M. (1989). The McGill action planning system (MAPS): A strategy for building the vision. *Journal of The Association for Persons with Severe Handicaps, 14*, 205–215.

Van der Klift, E., & Kunc, N. (1994). Beyond benevolence: Friendship and the politics of help. In J.S. Thousand, R. Villa, & A. Nevin (Eds.), *Creativity and collaborative learning* (pp. 391–401). Baltimore: Paul H. Brookes Publishing Co.

Appendix A

Blank Forms

Steps and Tools for Planning Individualized Adaptations

Step 1. Gather Information

    a. About the Student
- ❑ Student Information Form (confidential)
- ❑ Program-at-a-Glance

    b. About the Classroom
- ❑ Assessment of Classroom Procedures
- {❑} Assessment of Classroom Procedures: Detailed Ecological Assessment

Step 2. Determine When Adaptations are Needed
- {❑} Program Planning Matrix

Step 3. Decide on Planning Strategies
- ❑ Adaptations Planning Strategies Guide

Step 4. Plan and Implement General Adaptations
- ❑ Adaptations Plan   or   {❑} Classroom Participation Plan with General Adaptations

Step 5. Plan and Implement Specific Adaptations
- ❑ Weekly Plan for Specific Adaptations

Step 6. Plan and Implement Alternative Activities
- {❑} Lists or folders of alternative activities

Key: ({❑} Indicates Tools Typically Used Only for Students with Severe Disabilities)

Modifying Schoolwork, Janney & Snell, © 2000 Paul H. Brookes Publishing Co.

Student Information Form (Confidential)

Student _____ Grade _____ School Year _____

Current Teachers _____ Last Year's Teachers _____

Special Education & Related Services _____ Academics (list): _____ Speech: _____ Occupational Therapy: _____ Physical Therapy: _____ Aide Support: _____ Sp. Ed. Instruction: _____ Sp. Ed. Consultation: _____ Other:	**Likes** **Dislikes**
Medical/health	**See guidance counselor/ principal for other relevant confidential information?** _____ yes _____ no **Behavior Plan?** _____ yes (attach) _____ no
What works/learns best when **What does not work/ does not learn when**	**Other important information/ areas of concern**

Modifying Schoolwork, Janney & Snell, © 2000 Paul H. Brookes Publishing Co.

Program-at-a-Glance

Student _____ Date _____

IEP objectives	IEP accommodations

Academic/ social management needs	Comments/special needs

Assessment of Classroom Procedures

Subject/Grade Level _____ Date _____

Student _____ Teacher _____

	Instructional Activities	
Typical activities	**Frequently used student responses/tasks**	**Adaptations needed?**
Whole class		
Small groups		
Independent		

Homework (frequency and approximate duration)   **Adaptations?** _____

Textbooks, other frequently used materials   **Adaptations?** _____

General education teacher assistance   **Adaptations?** _____

Evaluation/testing   **Adaptations?** _____
Test/quiz format

Sources of information for tests

Rules, norms, routines   **Adaptations?** _____
Classroom rules and contingencies

Norms for student interaction and movement (talking, moving around the room, etc.)

Procedures for routines (lining up, handing in assignments, assigned jobs, etc.)

(Contributed by Johnna Elliott.)

Modifying Schoolwork, Janney & Snell, © 2000 Paul H. Brookes Publishing Co.

Assessment of Classroom Procedures: Detailed Ecological Assessment

Teacher _____ Class/Grade _____ Student _____
Subject _____ Activity _____ Time _____ Date _____

Typical sequence of steps/ procedures	Target student participation

Skills needed to increase participation

Adaptations needed to increase participation

(Contributed by Johnna Elliott.)

Modifying Schoolwork, Janney & Snell, © 2000 Paul H. Brookes Publishing Co.

Program Planning Matrix

Student _____ Class _____ Date _____

Class Schedule

IEP OBJECTIVES									

Modifying Schoolwork, Janney & Snell, © 2000 Paul H. Brookes Publishing Co.

Adaptations Planning Strategies Guide

Student   Class   Date

Classroom Teacher   **Special Education Teacher**

Meetings: **When?**   **How Long?**

Planning Format:

How will objectives be adapted?:   ____ Simplified   ____ Altered (functional/embedded skills)

Materials to be adapted:

____ worksheets ____ homework ____ textbook ____ study guides ____ quizzes/tests
____ other:

Plan for exchanging materials that need to be adapted:

Default plan: What will we do if either of us defaults on our responsibilities?
   Special education teacher:
   Classroom teacher:

Additional comments:

(Created from ideas contributed by Johnna Elliott and Cynthia Pitonyak.)

Modifying Schoolwork, Janney & Snell, © 2000 Paul H. Brookes Publishing Co.

Adaptations Plan

Student _____ Class _____ Date _____

Classroom Teacher _____ Special Education Teacher _____

Objectives _____

_____

Class activity	General adaptations	Specific adaptations*

* Specific adaptations developed during weekly planning meeting.
(Contributed by Johnna Elliott)

Modifying Schoolwork, Janney & Snell, © 2000 Paul H. Brookes Publishing Co.

Classroom Participation Plan with General Adaptations

Student _____ Class _____ Date _____

Curricular Adaptations _____

Activity	IEP objectives	General adaptations and procedures

Weekly Plan for Specific Adaptations (Secondary)

Student _____ Plan for week of _____

Teacher _____ Class _____

Class activity	Specific adaptations

(Contributed by Johnna Elliott.)

Modifying Schoolwork, Janney & Snell, © 2000 Paul H. Brookes Publishing Co.

Weekly Plan for Specific Adaptations

Student _____ Teacher/Class _____ Week of _____ Unit Theme _____

Subjects	Class objectives	Activities	Specific adaptations

Appendix B

Resources on Modifying Schoolwork

CREATING AN EFFECTIVE AND INCLUSIVE SCHOOL

Brandt, R.S. (1996). Creating a climate for learning [topical issue]. *Educational Leadership, 54*(1).

Developmental Studies Center. (1994). *At home in our schools: A guide to schoolwide activities that build community.* Oakland, CA: Author.

Developmental Studies Center. (1996). *Ways we want our class to be: Class meetings that build commitment to kindness and learning.* Oakland, CA: Author.

Kohn, A. (1996). *Beyond discipline: From compliance to community.* Alexandria, VA: Association for Supervision and Curriculum Development.

Kreidler, W.J. (1984). *Creative conflict resolution: More than 200 activities for keeping peace in the classroom.* Glenview, IL: Scott, Foresman & Company.

Schaps, E., & Solomon, D. (1990). Schools and classrooms as caring communities. *Educational Leadership, 48*(3), 38–42.

Solomon, D., Schaps, E., Watson, M., & Battistich, V. (1992). Creating caring school and classroom communities for all students. In R. Villa, J.S. Thousand, W. Stainback, & S. Stainback (Eds.), *Restructuring for caring and effective education* (pp. 41–60). Baltimore: Paul H. Brookes Publishing Co.

Van Dyke, R.E., Pitonyak, C.E., & Gilley, C.T. (1996). Planning, implementing, and evaluating inclusive education within the school. In L.A. Power-deFur & F.P. Orelove (Eds.), *Inclusive education: Practical implementation of the least restrictive environment* (pp. 27–41). Gaithersburg, MD: Aspen Publishers.

Villa, R.A., & Thousand, J.S. (Eds.). (2000). *Restructuring for caring and effective education: Piecing the puzzle together* (2nd ed.). Baltimore: Paul H. Brookes Publishing Co.

ACCOMMODATING CURRICULUM: INTEGRATED, THEMATIC, AND MULTICULTURAL CURRICULA

Dermon-Sparks, L. (1989). *Anti-bias curriculum: Tools for empowering young children.* Washington, DC: National Association for the Education of Young Children.

Kovalik, S. (1993). *Integrated thematic instruction: The model* (2nd ed.). Oak Creek, AZ: Books for Educators.

Marzano, R.J., Brandt, R.S., Hughes, C.S., Jones, B.F., Presseisen, B.Z., Rankin, S.C., & Suhor, C. (1988). *Dimensions of thinking.* Alexandria, VA: Association for Supervision and Curriculum Development.

McCracken, J.B. (1993). *Valuing diversity: The primary years.* Washington, DC: National Association for the Education of Young Children.

Parry, J., & Hornsby, D. (1985). *Write on: A conference approach to writing.* Portsmouth, NH: Heinemann.

ACCOMMODATING INSTRUCTIONAL PRACTICES: LEARNING STYLES, MULTIPLE INTELLIGENCES, LEARNING STRATEGIES, COOPERATIVE LEARNING, AND PEER TUTORING

Armstrong, T. (1994). *Multiple intelligences in the classroom.* Alexandria, VA: Association for Supervision and Curriculum Development.

Carbo, M.R., Dunn, R., & Dunn, K. (1986). *Teaching students to read through their individual learning styles.* Englewood Cliffs, NJ: Prentice-Hall.

Cohen, E.G. (1994). *Designing group work: Strategies for the heterogeneous classroom.* New York: Teachers College Press.

Deschler, D., & Schumaker, J.B. (1988). An instructional model for teaching students how to learn. In J. Graden, J. Zing, & M. Curtis (Eds.), *Alternative education delivery systems: Enhancing instructional options for all students* (pp. 391–411). Washington, DC: National Association for School Psychologists.

Dunn, R., & Dunn, K. (1992). *Teaching secondary students through their individual learning styles.* Boston: Allyn & Bacon.

Gardner, H. (1983). *Frames of mind: The theory of multiple intelligences.* New York: Basic Books.

Johnson, D.W., & Johnson, R. (1991). *Learning together and alone: Cooperation, competition, and individualization* (3rd ed.). Englewood Cliffs, NJ: Prentice-Hall.

Miller, L. (1993). *What we call smart.* San Diego: Singular.

Pressley, M., Burkell, J., Cariglia-Bull, T., Lysynchuk, L., McGoldrick, J.A., Schneider, B., Snyder, B., Symons, S., & Woloshyn, V.E. (1990). *Cognitive strategy instruction that really improves children's academic performance.* Cambridge, MA: Brookline.

Putnam, J.W. (Ed.). (1998). *Cooperative learning and strategies for inclusion: Celebrating diversity in the classroom* (2nd ed.). Baltimore: Paul H. Brookes Publishing Co.

Rhodes, L.K., & Dudley-Marling, C. (1988). *Readers and writers with a difference: A holistic approach to teaching learning disabled and remedial students.* Portsmouth, NH: Heinemann.

Tomlinson, C.A. (1995). *How to differentiate instruction in mixed-ability classrooms.* Alexandria, VA:

Association for Supervision and Curriculum Development.

INDIVIDUALIZED ADAPTATIONS, ACCOMMODATIONS, AND ALTERNATIVE INSTRUCTION

Elliott, J.R. (1996). Strategies for including students in elementary school programs. In L.A. Power-deFur & F.P. Orelove (Eds.), *Inclusive education: Practical implementation of the least restrictive environment* (pp. 153–166). Gaithersburg, MD: Aspen Publishers.

Falvey, M.A. (1995). *Inclusive and heterogeneous schooling: Assessment, curriculum, & instruction.* Baltimore: Paul H. Brookes Publishing Co.

Giangreco, M.F., Cloninger, C.J., & Iverson, V.S. (1998). *Choosing options and accommodations for children (COACH): A guide to planning inclusive education.* Baltimore: Paul H. Brookes Publishing Co.

Peterson, M., LeRoy, B., Field, S., & Wood, P. (1992). Community-referenced learning in inclusive schools. In S. Stainback & W. Stainback (Eds.), *Curriculum considerations in inclusive classrooms* (pp. 207–227). Baltimore: Paul H. Brookes Publishing Co.

Rainforth, B., York, J., & Macdonald, C. (1992). *Collaborative teams for students with severe disabilities.* Baltimore: Paul H. Brookes Publishing Co.

ALTERNATIVE AND ADAPTED EVALUATION PROCEDURES

Brandt, R. (1996–1997). On authentic performance assessment [topical issue]. *Educational Leadership, 54*(4).

Burke, K. (1994). *How to assess authentic learning.* Arlington Heights, IL: Skylight Training and Publishing.

Wolf, D.P. (1989, April). Portfolio assessment: Sampling student work. *Educational Leadership,* 35–39.

Wood, J., & Aldridge, J. (1985, March). Adapting tests for mainstreamed students. *Academic Therapy,* 419–426.

Index

Page numbers followed by "f" indicate figures; numbers followed by "t" indicate tables.

Teachers' Guides to Inclusive Practices!

These concise, issue-focused books from Martha E. Snell, Ph.D., and Rachel Janney, Ph.D., provide general and special educators with a bridge from inclusion research to inclusive practice, one subject at a time. Focusing on topics essential to inclusive school programs, each teacher-friendly guide briefly summarizes current research and recommended practices then outlines field-tested techniques for working with students who have disabilities. Completed sample forms and photocopiable blank forms accompany discussions of assessment, planning, implementation, and evaluation procedures for students of all ability levels in grades K–8.

Modifying Schoolwork

Full of proven strategies, this guidebook shows educators ways to adapt schoolwork to provide individualized attention to students with a broad range of learning and developmental disabilities.

Stock # 3548 • $25.00 • 2000 • 112 pages • 7 x 10 • paperback • ISBN 1-55766-354-8

Collaborative Teaming

This resource explains how to create successful education teams by building teamwork skills, developing problem-solving methods, implementing action plans, teaching collaboratively, and improving communication skills.

Stock # 353X • $25.00 • 2000 • 176 pages • 7 x 10 • paperback • ISBN 1-55766-353-X

Social Relationships and Peer Support

This guide offers effective strategies and programs that foster positive social relationships. Staff members will learn how to assess, develop, and teach skills that bolster formal and informal supportive friendships.

Stock # 3564 • $25.00 • 2000 • 208 pages • 7 x 10 • paperback • ISBN 1-55766-356-4

Behavioral Support

Educators will discover fresh, proactive ideas for helping students develop appropriate behavior skills, form positive relationships, and communicate effectively with peers and adults.

Stock # 3556 • $25.00 • 2000 • 120 pages • 7 x 10 • paperback • ISBN 1-55766-355-6